With Custer's Cavalry

General George Armstrong Custer, in hunting costume.

With Custer's Cavalry

by Katherine Gibson Fougera

From the memoirs of the late Katherine
Gibson, widow of Captain Francis M.
Gibson of the Seventh Cavalry, U. S. A.
(Retired). Illustrated with photographs.

University of Nebraska Press
Lincoln and London

First Bison printing: 1986
Most recent printing indicated by the first digit below:
    2   3   4   5   6   7   8   9   10

Library of Congress Cataloging-in-Publication Data
Fougera, Katherine Gibson, b. 1882.
  With Custer's cavalry.
  Reprint. Originally published: Caldwell, Idaho:
Caxton Printers, 1942.
  1. Gibson, Katherine, 1853–1934. 2. Gibson,
Francis M. 3. United States. Army—Military life.
4. Custer, George Armstrong, 1839–1876. 5. Little
Big Horn, Battle of the, 1876. 6. Pioneers—West
(U.S.)—Biography. 7. Women pioneers—West (U.S.)—
Biography. I. Title.
F594.G43F68 1986   973.8'092'2   86-4307
ISBN 0-8032-1973-3
ISBN 0-8032-6860-2 (pbk.)

Reprinted by arrangement with The Caxton Printers, Ltd.,
Caldwell, Idaho

DEDICATED TO THE MEMORY
OF
ELIZABETH B. CUSTER

Acknowledgment

✗

I wish to express my appreciation to John Shanahan for so ably reproducing, from faded originals, the photographs contained in this book.

KATHERINE GIBSON FOUGERA

Table of Contents

✗

List of Illustrations

✗

With Custer's Cavalry

By Train to Dakota

i

RISING ABOVE today's rich fields of golden grain throughout Kansas and the Dakotas, mirages of forgotten army posts, with their shadowy flags flapping in the crisp, dry breeze, dominate the sun-baked parade grounds of bygone days. Here one hears, midst faintly echoing bugle calls, the eerie neighing of spectral horses resounding from dilapidated cavalry stables. Ghostly fingers of wraiths in obsolete army uniforms are grasping luminous sabers, the points of which are tracing across rotting, alkali-dust-laden floors of abandoned barracks, new-old data, designed primarily to stress the intimate life and vicissitudes of the pioneer garrisons, rather than add to the already overwritten pages of Western history.

A few years prior to the Custer Massacre, my elder sister, Mollie Garrett, had married Lieutenant Donald McIntosh of the Seventh Cavalry, which regiment paused briefly at the sundry cavalry posts dotting the plains all the way from Oklahoma to the Dakotas. It intrigued us quite a bit, back in Washington, D. C., to learn that my brother-in-law's troop had changed stations nine times in eleven months, and my mother's stationary soul suffered acutely at the thought of Mollie's perpetual home making and breaking. However, she

failed to realize that large furniture, heavy draperies, and huge trunks stuffed with antiquated
finery played no part in her daughter's military
life and that strikers—soldier housemen, in army
parlance—could shove the entire contents of an
officer's quarters into a government truck and the
regiment be on the march in less than two hours.

My own advent upon this active scene came about
unexpectedly, and, as sometimes events of importance turn upon the merest trifles, so destiny chose
to fling me into a totally different world, by way
of a conventional piece of wearing apparel. I refer
to the atrocious all-enveloping crepe veil so rigidly
adhered to in the long ago, which made the wearer
look like an animated black ghost, and frightened
children and horses. This I donned on the death of
my father and straightway developed a persistent
cough. The insistence of the doctor that I discard
the crowlike, air-excluding horror threw my family
into a state of consternation.

"For what will the church and people say?"
asked my lady-mother plaintively.

"And our pew is so conspicuously located,"
wailed Sister Sally, who talked like a book.

My mother nodded. "But we might change it,"
she amended hopefully.

"Yes—or even the church," added my sister.

"But there's your Aunt Olive," pursued the
former gloomily. "She is so easily upset."

Sister Sally sighed. "And think of our neighbors—such an unprecedented laxity of mourning
conventions. Well——"

They surveyed me gravely and I, plucking nervously at my black bead necklace, felt like a pariah. Suddenly I blurted out, "Well, why can't I go out to Mollie?" and unloosed a hollow cough. That settled it, for my mother gave me a swift, startled look, hurried to her desk, and that very day her letter was speeding West.

The day of my great adventure arrived, and escorted to the railroad station by a cortege of friends and relatives, some smiling, some sniveling, I climbed aboard the car.

"Remember your cod-liver oil," counseled my mother, and, irrelevantly, "your gentle breeding."

"And permit no license of speech or touch from strangers," admonished Sister Sally in flowery vein.

"An' Honey Chile, don' you get tangled up with no Injun chief," quavered black Mammy Lindy, her lip beginning to tremble.

Once inside and my luggage installed, I flew to the window and waved good-by to my family and bawling Mammy. Conflicting emotions assailed me, for while my heart sang in anticipation of the trip, my eyes misted as the slowly moving train slid away from the platform, and the faces of my dear ones began to dim and blur, finally vanishing entirely. Even the fleet bare feet of Mammy's thieving son, George, sprinting after the train were left behind, and suddenly I felt forlorn. For ten minutes I permitted myself to be supremely miserable, then I dabbed my eyes with my black-edged handkerchief and looked around. On the seat facing me appeared a huge traveling bag marked "Louisiana," seemingly ownerless. I was just going to speak to the porter about it when a dapper little man in a wide-trousered linen suit paused beside me. He bowed stiffly and addressed me in stilted English.

"Pardon, Mademoiselle, but permit me to present myself. I am Jean Baptiste Bois, of New Orleans—at your service." He bobbed up and down like a cork. "I rejoice that we are to occupy the same compartment."

I smiled at him cautiously, recalling Sister Sally's license advice, nodded primly, and said nothing. Thus rebuffed, he betook himself to another part of the train, and I had practically the whole section to myself. Then I opened the bag and extracted my linen duster, which I promptly donned against the ravages of coal dust, already sifting through the car window. Unpinning my mourning veil, I stuffed it in my valise. The rest of the time passed uneventfully, and at the end of a tiring day I turned into the lower berth early.

Naturally, I awoke with the larks and, thinking to precede the mob which would soon bombard the ladies' dressing room, I reached up in the semidarkness for my duster, which I threw across my shoulders, groped for my bag, and stole into the washroom.

In a few minutes I heard a rap at the door and the porter's voice drawling apologetically, " 'Scuse me, Miss, but de French gent'man say you got on his pants."

In the act of brushing my teeth I hissed through the door. "Tell him I haven't," and he shambled away. But not for long.

Back he came and funneled through the door crack, "Please, lady, de French gent'man 'sists you-all has his pants, an' he wants 'em."

My hairbrush was just descending on my scalp, but I paused with it in midair. This was becoming annoying, so I replied with asperity, "You tell him that he is mistaken, and don't annoy me again."

The very idea of that impudent foreigner attempting to bother me like that—the very idea! The brush ploughed viciously through my hair. But the end was not yet because, just as I had finished slipping into my dress, back came the dusky disturber.

"I'se powerfully sorry, Miss, but de gent'man say you suttenly has on his pants, and dey's five hundred dollars in 'em," he explained reluctantly.

By this time I was furious, and, throwing my duster over my shoulders, I flung open the door and sailed into the aisle, head held high and explosive words on the tip of my tongue. To my embarrassment every head was poked inquisitively through its curtains, and all eyes were fixed upon me.

As I approached my section there sat the Frenchman in the upper berth, yelling excitedly, "Look—see—she have on my pants. I see her take zem."

Petrified with sudden apprehension, I glanced down at myself and discovered that my duster had mysteriously changed into a pair of wide linen trousers. I felt myself pale, then turn fiery red as I realized that in my haste in the semidarkness I had yanked the trousers instead of my duster off the rail. How careless and stupid I had been! Perhaps these people thought that I had intended to steal that money. Maybe that man would have me arrested. My hand went swiftly to my throat. What would I do? What could I do?

And then I heard the first chuckle, followed by another and another, until the car was rocking with merriment, and an older woman said kindly, "Don't look so frightened, child. Everyone makes mistakes sometimes."

I teetered between laughter and tears but refrained from either. I merely removed the troublesome trousers from around my neck and handed them to Monsieur Bois with an apologetic, "Oh, I'm so sorry, Monsieur. Please forgive my stupidity." And, of course, he did, most gallantly.

He even invited me to have breakfast with him, which I accepted brazenly, but, I defended myself defiantly, I was committing no crime. Besides, I was launched upon the road of high adventure. It was a good breakfast, too, over which we grew quite chummy. I even unbent sufficiently to tell him my name, while he propounded the intricacies of sugar refining, which happened to be his business. So he really turned out to be quite nice, and when he left the train a few hours later I missed him.

By this time we were headed well into the Middle West, and the temperature had lowered.

Pretty farms began to appear with their tucked-
in fields, green and prosperous looking, while white
frame churches and red-roofed schoolhouses dotted
the land. I sat by the window for hours gazing
upon these peaceful rustic scenes.

Finally we reached Chicago, the gateway of the
real West, of which Mollie had written. As I
crossed the town a chill breeze explored my clothing, and I wrapped my coat closer about me, then
I began to spread my focus.

There was an air of newness about this town,
which seemed to stretch out jerkily between crowded blocks, followed by empty spaces; then habitations would appear again. Many were comparatively new, presenting façades of limestone, brick,
sandstone, and even marble, besides which, curiously enough, were huddled tumbled-down shan-
ties. The types of humanity here must have hailed
from every country under the sun, the sturdy,
pale-haired Scandinavians predominating. Their
rosy-cheeked, white-skinned women, whose yellow
hair escaped from beneath bright-colored handkerchiefs and blew across their blue eyes, were busy
carrying baskets of food supplies hither and yon.
Rangy cowboys rode big-boned horses and wore
their sombreros rakishly, and I saw my first Indian right on the pavement of this windy city. A
war bonnet capped his straight black hair and
zigzagged down his lean, bare back. Shabby buckskin trousers encased his thin, long legs, and his
agile feet, moccasin clad, were executing rhythmic,
pounding steps interspersed by sudden leaps into

the air, accompanied by occasional whoops and droning minor sounds supplied by a bareheaded squaw. A huge basket of beadwork stood beside her, evidently for sale, and the side show had been staged for advertising purposes. I leaned out of the carriage window and watched them until we turned the corner, then I relaxed. This place reminded me of Washington—it was so different— and the dearth of negroes made me homesick.

I attained my train and lost no time in getting settled for my long jaunt on the Chicago and Northwestern Railroad. After leaving Chicago my young mind started on a voyage of make-believe. My compartment had become a theater box and the semiobscurity of the station, a stage curtain, which, as the train slowly nosed its way into the light, rose upon a drama of strange and interesting people and things. Soon we were passing through the outskirts of the town, abutting in a tail of hovels, and headed north, the locomotive picking up speed at every mile. On the level, downdale, we pounded, sometimes spanning streams that glittered with gold polka dots in the sunshine. Ranches popped up here and there, and the whiff of concentrated winter hay, drifting out of open barn doors and lofts, piqued the nostrils pleasantly. Herds of horses at pasture met the eye, and here the spring stork had been active. Young foals pushed their heads into pans of fodder or munched contentedly on a carrot or an apple, while the newly borns, straddled upon unsteady legs, rooted experimentally into the bellies of their dams.

As we approached the plains, the chill, champagne crispness in the air made me grateful for the warmth of the wood-burning stove, one of which was installed in each car. Spring seemed to be somewhat of a laggard in these parts, yet, judging from the covered wagons that loomed up at intervals on the horizon like white sails, it was evident that some dauntless souls shelved the question of climatic comforts as of little importance. At closer range these caravans, drawn by pairs of oxen, yoked together, evoked in me a lively interest, for they could almost be likened to tiny houses on wheels. Fairly long, they were built high for the purpose of floating down or across streams, thus serving as a protection for freight as well as human life. Hoop-shaped slats were cleated along the sides and arched over the center of the wagon, then strong canvas was drawn taut, thereby covering the entire body. The driver was usually a stern-looking, bearded man, though sometimes it was the sunbonneted, resolute-faced woman beside him who held the reins. It made no difference, and each one carried a carbine. The children and luggage occupied the wagon proper along with the household equipment, while a dog or two trotted beside the impromptu home. Inside, swinging in hammocks, babies slept contentedly.

A tremendous admiration welled in my heart for these courageous families. There was no hysteria in these women's make-up nor shifting expression in their calm, determined eyes, for they were real helpmates to their husbands, whom they must have loved with fathomless devotion to have accompanied them into this wilderness.

It was a far cry from Washington, D. C., to Fort Lincoln, Dakota, where my brother-in-law's troop was roosting, and it was a radical change from the torrid May weather hanging soggily over the Potomac to the clear ozone of the plains, but, like a plant thirsting for water, I gulped great lungfuls of it, and, almost magically, my cough vanished. Never having been far from home, I saw everything through wide, astonished eyes, and the farther west we penetrated the more I pictured myself as being in an alien world. It was an eerie sensation, this groping into the unknown, with human habitations stretching wider and wider apart. Great wastes of rippling sand left by the imprint of receding waves told tales of intimacy with the earth eons ago, the only evidence of plant life dotted here and there being the hardy cactus, stunted sage, and cedar brush, on which snow patches still lingered. My eyes fixed themselves abstractedly on the far horizon, and I pondered many things. What species of fish had once infested those inland seas or lakes? And had those waters been deep enough to have been influenced by lunar tides; and what about reptiles?

Here the thread of my musing snapped, for surely over there in the distance the sands were moving. I held my breath as we neared the spot, expecting I knew not what, but prepared for anything. I was right. Something was moving, but not the sands. It was merely a small, dust-colored

pony. What a letdown! Yet I was intrigued.
What would a pony be doing out there with nothing
edible in sight? My suspense was brief, for, rising
from behind a sizable cedar bush, loomed an Indian. Gaunt of face, capless, and wrapped in a
blanket, he stood like stone. The sight of him
startled me, because he was so different from the
gaily caparisoned one I saw in Chicago, and in
the moment that flashed between the moving train
and the red man, I noted a brooding expression in
his eyes as they followed us. From then on I was
to see many like him.

People were kind, perhaps because I was alone,
young, and none too robust-looking. I loved the
vastness of the prairies and the smell of buffalo
grass, and I was lost in admiration for the lithe,
tiptoe-swaying cowboy, loud of voice and laughter,
who smelled of horse hide and played cards most
of the time. My appetite picked up, and I ate beans
and beans and beans and tough, fresh-killed beef
with a relish that I never accorded Mammy Lindy's
delicious corn pone and fried chicken.

My fellow passengers were a cosmopolitan lot,
from the soft-spoken conductor hailing from the
South who quoted Shakespeare and had forgotten
the war was over, to mothers of restless broods en
route to join husbands and fathers who had preceded them and had started nest building in these
strange places. Then there were gimlet-eyed engineers who kept to themselves and figured eternally on paper, deciding where the next bridge,
road, or dam was to be constructed. Also there

were impassive-faced men with cold, appraising eyes, wearing imported English clothes, who might be suspected of being either Eastern bankers or the owners of these ambitious young roads.

The train moved leisurely and, though supposed to run on scheduled time, it rarely did. We might be from one to three hours late. It all depended on what was happening. Besides, in those days competition was not so keen. Hot boxes were common, delaying us from ten to thirty minutes sometimes. However, it gave us a chance to stretch our legs, the men crowding around the working crew, others taking pot shots at rabbits or gophers while the women and children gathered a few wild flowers or sunned themselves on the plain.

Once a herd of antelopes came within easy reach of a rifleshot from the car windows, and two Englishmen, in immaculate hunting togs and bound West in quest of big game, became almost apoplectic with excitement, so the conductor obligingly stopped the train for a little sport. Another time a buffalo calf suddenly appeared on the tracks, evidently separated from its herd, and was voicing its lamentations of fright and loneliness in no uncertain tones. As no shooing had the slightest effect on it, the engineer brought the train to a fifteen-minute stop, and, upon investigation, it was found that the stray one had caught its hoof in a rail. Once extricated, the baby scampered away, and we rolled on. However, no criticism flayed these irregularities. On the contrary, it almost seemed that they were welcomed, because they offered such splendid opportunities for gambling among the passengers. They bet on the chances of arriving early or late at the stations, and the one who guessed the nearest time either way won the money. In fact, this game provided the most exciting feature of the day's trip.

While all these events were more or less diverting, one would suddenly realize that hunger was gnawing at one's vitals, and the eating station might still be some miles away. And in regard to these stations, mere crude wooden shacks, the railroad displayed an astonishing inconsistency. While the officials were prone to humor the whims of the passengers, they became exacting when it came to feeding time. The train often paused at these shacks but a few minutes. Time had to be made up, it was claimed, and one might just be scalding one's mouth against a tin cup of coffee, or snatching a sandwich, when the whistle would blow, the conductor shout, "All aboard!" and we would have to scamper back to our car or be left behind. The result was a food stampede. Feet were trampled on, right and left, timid people jostled out of the way, and human nature in the raw gave a good imitation of the bad behavior of its child-primitive man. In one instance a worn mother with four ravenous urchins grabbed a sizzling steak in a piece of paper on her hurried way to the train, when a lean, hungry-looking Cassius in top boots, wide-brimmed hat, and chaps tried to snatch it right out of her hand. Whereupon another burly stranger, similarly clad, promptly knocked him down, salvaged the tidbit from the alkali dust, and returned it to the bewildered woman.

My first experience with this food-grabbing game was when I found myself being literally carried towards the eating shack by the impact of bodies behind me. Here I glimpsed a sawdust-covered floor, a big stove in the center of the room, and five or six brigandish-looking men around it, chewing tobacco, while on the side stood a huge table groaning with bread, ham, potatoes, pies, and steaming cans of coffee, whereupon several hundred hands reached out over my head, and before I knew it, I felt my small person being propelled away beyond the appetizing board. Just then the whistle blew, and I ran for the train, and when, breathless, I flung myself aboard, I discovered that I had purloined only a handful of pickles. I could have cried with disappointment because I was so hungry. However, the cowboy who had done battle for the steak offered me a soggy biscuit, bitter from an overdose of baking powder. This I accepted gratefully and devoured with the pickles.

Of course, during the so-called lunch hour, the train was completely deserted, and, out on an empty prairie, no one could imagine anything happening to it. However, as with hat tilted over my nose through the careless gesture of some hasty hand and my thin elbow keeping at bay a two-hundred-pound female who was intent upon snatching the only remaining piece of pie upon which I had centered my eye, I heard noise and commotion issuing from the car. Fearing that it was about to pull out without me, I scooped up the pastry, flung a quarter on the counter, and scurried back to the train. Here, amid shouts and threats, I saw two cowboys being held by some of the crew, who were tying the wrists of the prisoners with rope.

"What happened?" I asked of the battling one who chanced to be standing near.

"Why," said he, "while we was off feedin', a couple of low-down cowpunchers tried to make off with the stove in Number 3."

"But," I argued, "it was lighted."

"That ain't nothin', Ma'am. They jest yanked the chimney free, then they was carryin' the stove right onto the station platform on t'other side, when the engineer come along and ketched 'em."

"Still," I persisted, for it didn't make sense to me, "it *was* lighted."

He flung me a pitying glance for my dumbness and walked away.

Hovering about the rough pine wood huts serving as railroad stations appeared picturesque, sloe-eyed squaws carrying baskets of moccasins and other embroidered buckskin merchandise, while shy-faced children clung to them, all waiting for the iron horse and hoping to sell their wares. I purchased a couple of articles, then, spying a cute, slate-eyed papoose, I swooped him up impulsively from the bag on his mother's back and held him close in my arms. The little rascal snuggled his nose under my neck, and I gave him

a big squeeze. Then my blue eyes met the black
ones of his mother, and we both smiled. A novel
situation—with the tribesmen of one woman already mapping out warpaths to entrap the un-
wary white man and the men of my race preparing
a campaign to wipe out the redskins. I sighed
and returned the wee one to the squaw just as the
conductor called, "All aboard," but I decided that
the psychology applying to the red and white men
was beyond fathoming by my humble grey matter,
so I shelved it. As I waved good-by, the squaw's
eyes followed me wistfully.

My original plan was to meet Mollie at Fort
Pierre, Dakota, where we would take the steamer
up the Missouri to Bismarck, not far from Fort
Lincoln, but heavy rainfalls and thawing snows
had swollen the river until it had overflowed its
banks, so we abandoned this idea and selected Columbia, Dakota, for our rendezvous instead. While
the change of scheme entailed a long ride by coach
before we could reach a shoot of the Northern Pacific Railroad at Grand Rapids, Dakota, and would
take us farther out of our way, by way of Fargo,
it was less dangerous. The elements were still on
the rampage, for as we crawled across the Dakota
territory line a terrific wind tore at the train,
rocking it against the rails. The temperature
dropped sharply, and torrents of sleet lashed furi-
ously at the windowpanes, while drops of water
rolled down the chimney and fell into the stove
with a hiss.

Unused to such climatic foment, I turned to my

square-headed, square-shouldered seat companion. "Is—is this a tornado?" I quavered timidly.

A row of gold teeth worth a ransom flashed through a wide-mouthed smile, and a kindly nasal voice, punctuated by imperfect grammar, replied, "No, sister—'tain't nothin' but a little gale." And at that moment the train swayed violently, bouncing us together like a couple of marbles.

I retrieved myself and shrank farther into my winter coat, chilled to the bone. Presently a large, pudgy hand thrust a flask under my nose, and again I faced the opulent smile.

"Take a swig, sister. You look blue about the gills."

My acquaintance with alcohol began and ended with blackberry cordial, my mother's panacea for overindulgence at Thanksgiving, Christmas, and green-apple time. However, outside the eating stations, I tried to remember that I was supposed to be well-bred, so I took the flask, minus cup, with a dubious smile, sniffed the contents, and hesitated.

"Go right ahead, sister. I ain't afeared to drink after you," assured the unknown magnanimously.

Thus urged, I tipped the bottle and took a big gulp. Senses and sorrows! When that firewater struck my stomach it galvanized me like a shot of nitroglycerin. I coughed, I sneezed, I hiccoughed. I thrust the flask back into the fat paw, clapped my hand over my mouth, and fled to the water cooler. After the burning thirst had been appeased I navigated back to my seat and sat down heavily. But, after a while, a peculiar lightness seemed to float right into my brain—due to the jerky motion of the train, no doubt—and then, suddenly, to my surprise I began to titter inanely and felt oddly reckless.

"It's so funny," I giggled.

"What's funny?" queried my fat friend.

"Oh, everything," airily, "you and I and the train and those black cats in the distance," waving my hand towards the window.

"Hey, them cats is buffalo herds," he contradicted, adding, "Just one drink, sister, but you've sure got a skinful."

Then I became drowsy, and I must have fallen asleep, because later, when the train jerked to a grinding stop, I opened my eyes dazedly and gazed around. Luggage had been dislodged and children hurled sprawling to the floor, where they rubbed bumped heads and bawled lustily.

Unconsciously my hand strayed to my neck where it rested on something rough but familiar. Good Heavens! The crepe veil was draped across my shoulders. I gazed at it, astonished. How and when and why had that popped up again? I hadn't touched it, to my recollection, since I stowed it away in my valise the day I left Washington. It puzzled me, but so did other things—my uneasy head, dry mouth, and throat, and gradually the meaning of "skinful" began to penetrate my skull. I felt the color flow upward from my neck. One gulp, I mused, but I must have swallowed half the bottle.

Shades of my conservative ancestors! First I

picked up with sundry strange men on trains, and now I had imbibed too freely of the grain. At this rate, according to Sister Sally, had she known about it, I would be well on my way to the gutter. Unpleasant thought, yet I found my mind wrestling with the problem of the veil primarily. Possibly I had grown chilly in my befuddled sleep and subconsciously had pulled it out for extra covering, and, as though to prove the accuracy of my deduction, my bag was wide open.

For a moment I was sunk in confusion, but finally my curiosity struggled to the surface, and I turned to my companion, hidden behind a two-months-old newspaper.

"Why are we stopping?" I asked.

He looked at me and grinned.

"Just another hot box," and his bulging eyes regarded me knowingly. Again the color flooded my cheeks, and I looked down. Soon I felt a beefy hand patting mine awkwardly.

" 'Tain't nothin', sister," the nasal voice assured me. "Nobody's agoin' to hold it agin you, and likely it done you a power of good. Here, take another swig."

"Oh, no, thank you," I declined hastily, and suddenly we both laughed. From that day until he left the train this side of Columbia, I never had to hustle for a meal, because he always brought back enough for us both, though I insisted upon paying my share.

Gradually the passengers dropped off at the different stations, and but a few got on. Finally on my last night on the train I had practically the whole car to myself.

I turned in early to get a good sleep, but, because of excitement, perhaps, or maybe because the moon was so bright and silvery white, I lay looking out upon that vast wilderness for hours, my eyes picking out solitary ranches which stood out bleakly from time to time in the pale light as the miles spun behind us. Great empty spaces from the human viewpoint, yet no magic wand had changed into thin air the thousands of buffaloes and antelopes, skipping rabbits, and slithering coyotes and gophers that scuddled or padded across these plains. An awareness of stirring nature crept over me though the land lay as peaceful as an uninhabited planet. But was it really so tranquil? As if in answer to my unspoken query, off in the distance against a cold, glittering background of stars, a ragged row of conelike shapes began to dot the sky line, looking larger as the train approached. Suddenly I realized what the puzzling objects were—tepees, built of buffalo skins, lashed together with leather thongs and stretched over poles. Tepees, starkly real, with moving, picketed forms hovering near. Ponies, doubtless, and a dog or two barked faintly out of the stillness. These signs spelled Indians and plenty of them. How mutable is the human mind, for these villages of which I had seen many every day, with their picturesque filth, had ceased to intrigue me, yet now, at the sight of them, I suddenly sensed a curious uneasiness and mentally shook myself. Had lunar witchery laid hold of my imagination, or was the unfamiliar nocturnal setting lending an eerie note to disturb me? The moon was sliding slowly down the sky, and in the hills a coyote screamed. I shivered a little, closed my eyes, crept under the blankets, and then, for no reason in particular, thought of Mollie's husband, Lieutenant McIntosh of Custer's fighting Seventh, and the year was 1874.

The night dragged on, and from time to time the train squeaked to a stop. Once several passengers got on, and, as they passed my berth, I caught snatches of conversation delivered to the porter in rumbling whispers.

"Yep," someone was saying, "Doc Wilson and his gang grabbed a big haul tonight when they held up that stagecoach."

"Sho 'nough?" queried the negro with bated breath.

"So they sez, and——" here the voices trailed away, but my heart beat faster. A holdup. I had read of such things, but to be within comparatively few miles of the actual happening was disquieting, and at that moment I longed fervently to be home with my lady-mother. Hours afterwards, it seemed to me, I fell into an exhausted sleep and only awakened when a drawling voice spoke outside my curtains.

"Here, Missy, I brung you some coffee and aiggs, and a hunk er bread," said the porter, who looked like Mammy's thieving son George.

"Oh," I exclaimed, sitting up in the berth, "how

nice of you," and when a battered tin plate was poked through the curtain flap I fell upon the tasteless coffee, hard fried eggs, and stale bread with the appetite of a hired man.

Later I discovered that the porter, myself, and a lean, square-jawed cowboy, clean shaven and as straight as an Indian, were the sole occupants of the car.

"Unique," I asked the porter, that being his name, "what became of the other men who got on last night?"

"Oh, dey got off at de breakfast station, ma'am, 'cept him," nodding towards the stranger.

"Was it true that a bandit and his gang held up the stage near where we were last night?"

"Yas'um—dey do say so."

"But why do the people out here permit such outrages?" I demanded, tossing my head with indignation.

"'Cause dey jest cain't ketch dat Doc Wilson."

"Why not?" I persisted, "with plenty of soldiers and law-abiding cowboys ready to protect the lives and property of the settlers." I glanced furtively at my other car companion, hoping that my flattering reference to his fraternity might quicken his interest, because he was nice-looking, and I was young and very blonde, and we had still some miles to travel before we reached Columbia. But his head was buried behind a newspaper; in fact, newspaper absorption out there seemed to be a passion, no matter how old the news happened to be.

"'Cause, ma'am," Unique was explaining, "dey always wears masquerade."

"You mean masks?"

"Yas'um—one of dem things dat covers de face."

"Oh, I see, a sort of Robin Hood and his merry men."

"Yas'um—no, ma'am."

I caught a fleeting glimpse of the cowboy's face and sensed that he was amused. That was encouraging, so I continued trying to impress him with my knowledge.

"Do you know who Robin Hood was?" I asked.

"No, ma'am, not 'zactly."

"Well, he was a good bandit and only robbed to help the poor, and he was the protector of women and children."

The negro's eyes bulged. "Sho 'nough?"

I nodded. "And he lived—er—lived," I floundered, "well, many years ago."

Unique wagged his head sagely. "Yas'um," he agreed, "lots of things happened de time of de Civil War," and he proceeded to stuff a pillow into its case.

WE WERE SCHEDULED to reach Columbia at ten o'clock in the morning, but, of course, we would be a couple of hours late, so, paying no further attention to my unresponsive cowboy, I drifted into a much-needed sleep.

It seemed that I had hardly taken forty winks when Unique touched me on the arm.

" 'Scuse me, Miss, but ain't you-all gettin' off at Columbia?"

"Yes," I replied impatiently, "but why wake me now?"

" 'Cause we is yere." I glanced hurriedly at my watch.

"Impossible," I ejaculated. "It's only ten o'clock."

"Cain't help it, ma'am. We's on time."

On time—it was the first instance of schedule regularity since we left Chicago. No wonder I was fussed and dropped my purse and gloves and pushed my poke bonnet awry.

Unique was reaching leisurely for my valise when the unsociable cowboy swung into the aisle and bore down upon us with rapid strides. His strong bronzed fingers flicked the porter aside as though he were a fly, then, tossing a tawny lock of hair out of his steel-blue eyes, he picked up my two pieces of luggage and strode to the platform of the car, where he deposited them. Then he returned to his own seat and gathered up a roll of buffalo robes, which he hauled out and dumped beside my things. The incident, the total silence, so bewildered me that I almost forgot to tip Unique, who gaped, open-mouthed, after the self-appointed helper.

The train rocked to a stop, and I was just stammering my thanks to the latter when I glimpsed a tall figure mincing restlessly up and down on feet too small for her, in front of a ramshackle frame station. At sight of Mollie's cameo features and her handsome head tilted back at its familiar angle, my throat choked up, and in one jump I was off that train, and two more carried me straight into her arms. Forgotten was the cowboy and the luggage while for a moment we clung together, both of us supplying the home links we hungered for. How good it was to see her! The sun flashed on her white, even teeth as she smiled and asked a thousand breathless questions.

Meanwhile the few remaining passengers, consisting of ranchmen and cowpunchers, were trickling out of the train and approaching some horses tethered to a long rope stretched between poles. The creatures whinnied their welcome and pawed the ground joyously while their masters untied their halters, then flung themselves across the animals' flanks and clattered off.

"Any luggage, ma'am?" inquired a deep voice at my elbow, bringing us out of our family huddle.

I whirled and encountered the bovine eyes of a roughly dressed stranger, wearing a fur cap with ear tabs and affecting a walrus mustache that moved up and down when he talked. I suppose it was this latest bit of queerness that punctured my overwrought nerves, for I began to laugh hysterically, and the blanker the poor man looked, the more I chortled. May, the fur cap, the meandering mustache. It was too much.

Finally Mollie broke in somewhat sternly, "It is often very cold out here in May, particularly when driving at night, and this is our driver who is to take us to the railroad—in that stage over there."

This extinguished my levity, and I was immediately contrite. In fact, I was about to apologize, but Mollie shook her head, so I let it pass and turned my attention to "that stage over there." Standing at a short distance away, high, cumbersome, uncomfortable-looking, and drawn by four heavy horses, it might have seen service during the Civil War or even before.

"Any luggage, ma'am?" repeated the driver, apparently without resentment.

"Yes, luggage," echoed Mollie, suddenly alert.

"Luggage," I re-echoed, abruptly remembering, then I smiled. "Of course. There it is," pointing toward the coach, "and my trunk I sent by express."

Sure enough, my cavalier of the train had just reached the old vehicle, into which he was stowing my belongings as well as his own. In the bright

sunlight he was good to look upon, all in brown
from the tip of his swanky sombrero to the soles
of his leather boots. Even his two gun cases fitted
into the color scheme of his flannel shirt and his
tan- and gravy-toned handkerchief about his neck.
Then I saw Mollie stiffen, and I remembered certain idiosyncracies peculiar to her alone, one of
which was her pet aversion to brown—any brown.
In short, when she saw brown, she saw red.
Strange, but true, and no person this side of
Heaven could change her, so when she said, "Who
is that man in snuffy brown?" all hopes of having
a pleasant conversation with the useful stranger
went aglimmering.

Notwithstanding, I smiled at him a bit self-
consciously and remarked, "Thanks for your
trouble."

Mollie gave me a swift glance and climbed into
the coach. The cowboy dismissed my indebtedness
with an expansive sweep of his lean hand and
helped me into the stage. He followed and seated
himself on the extreme opposite side, where he immediately dived behind the inevitable newspaper.

The driver unhitched his horses, climbed upon
his seat, cracked his whip, and we were on our
way.

Our antiquated conveyance accommodated nine
persons. Like the covered wagon, it was built high
off the ground for the purpose of stream fording
and had open canvas sides which were fastened
down with buttons. While they kept out the sun
in mild weather, they also tore away from their

moorings and flapped eerily like ghost draperies, when the prairie gods loosed their devastating wind and sand storms in this land of violence. Springs? There were none, as I was to learn shortly, when the old wheels sagged first into one jagged rut, then another, knocking us together like tennis balls. Because I was small and light of weight, my brain reeled occasionally when my head collided unexpectedly with the top of the diligence. I rubbed it ruefully, but received no sympathy from Mollie.

"Good for your liver," she jerked out, as she lunged against me. Notwithstanding our liver churning and discomfort, we lapsed, of course, into an orgy of news and reminiscences, while we clung fiercely to the swinging straps as the stage careened through clogged roads, or rather wagon trails. By way of news I gasped out sentences, hanging on to the seat.

"J-i-m H-a-r-r-i-s i-s d-e-a-d."

"J-i-m H-a-r-r-i-s?" echoed Mollie. "T-o-o b-a-d."

"Yes, S-i-s-t-e-r S-a-l-l-y was greatly u-p-s-e-t over the loss of her o-l-d b-e-a-u."

"H-E-R b-e-a-u," mocked Mollie angrily. "R-I-D-I-C-U-L-O-U-S! He was M-I-N-E. Proposed f-i-r-s-t night—met m-e—beside s-o-f-a—trod on y-o-u-r d-o-l-l."

Here our unsociable companion uttered a sudden chuckle. Why, he was human after all, but Mollie withered him with a glance, and he subsided.

As for me, it saddened me to recall those good old family days when my young lady sisters rowed continuously over their admirers.

Once Mollie playfully slapped Sister Sally in the face, where a spring boil was ripening. Sally fainted, and, thinking her dead, I screamed. Ours was a lively household.

After that our cowboy resumed his indifferent attitude; in fact, we didn't exist as far as he was concerned.

Donald, it seemed, had intended to accompany Mollie on her trip to Columbia, but the garrison received sudden orders to be in readiness for a visit from the Inspector; and General Custer, in command, during the absence of General Sturgis, had canceled all leaves.

"So," complained Mollie, "I had to come alone and spend the night in that awful hole called an inn at Columbia."

"What a shame," I protested indignantly. "It's a pity the General can't spare one officer out of his whole regiment for a couple of days."

Mollie surveyed me coolly. "Don't be silly," she counseled caustically. Being habitually rebuffed by my older sisters left me somewhat callous to their criticisms; besides, I caught a glint of strong teeth behind an amused smile as my cavalier rattled his paper, so I was emboldened to persist.

"I am at a loss to conjecture," I began airily, aping Sister Sally, "why you tolerate such regulation of your domestic affairs."

That burst of oratory was spontaneous, and I

was proud of it, but Mollie seared me with, "Stop showing off."

And did I subside? Crimson to the ears, I flopped back heavily against the ancient cushions, thereby releasing from cracks and oozing holes in the upholstery quantities of dust which settled upon me and made me cough.

Silence engulfed the three of us, broken from time to time by the four or five tuneful notes of the meadow lark which flew up out of the grass at our approach. The sun came out in glaring radiance, and one could almost see the few little patches of snow melting, while half-grown grasshoppers leaped gaily into the stage and perched upon our laps. I picked as many as I could out of the seat, but when I saw that neither Mollie nor the cowboy paid the slightest attention to them, I just let them ride.

Indians, single and in small groups, began to appear more frequently. Tempted by the promising weather, some young bucks had discarded their blankets, revealing bare, red-brown bodies seated astride their ponies. Breech cloths girded their loins, from which pended a tomahawk. A few of them carried bows, while arrows stuck out of bags on their backs. In broad daylight and in small numbers I could study these savages dispassionately and without fear, especially as the driver, cowboy, and even Mollie—to my surprise—toted guns.

I noted among other things that, while the high cheekbones and straight black hair claimed kin-

ship with the Mongolian race, still this strain must
have forked somewhere to account for the red skins
and non-slant eyes. Another point of interest was
the muscular arms and legs that seemed too thin
for their bodies. Their bodies swayed like reeds
in the wind to every movement of their fast little
ponies.

Our progress over those rutted trails was so slow
that at times our horses literally walked, and it
was during one of these periods of almost suspended animation that something happened. At
one end of a fallen log, lying fairly close to the
road, perched a meadow lark which had evidently
been sunning itself, but it was its attitude that
drew my attention. It was standing with wings
outstretched as though poised for flight, yet its
feet seemed rooted to the bark, as its startled gaze
rested upon some object. My own glance followed
the bird's, and my blood chilled, for a long, slithering shape was undulating slowly along the top of
the log, moving closer and closer to the lark, which
its beady, hypnotic eyes held prisoner in a web of
terror.

"Oh," I ejaculated hysterically, pointing, "the
snake!"

Both Mollie and the cowboy started, the hand
of the latter dropping swiftly to one of his guns.
Instantly he trained its blue muzzle on the log, and,
before one could draw a breath, a bullet had drilled
that reptile, decapitating it as neatly as though
cleaved with an axe.

I fell back again with a sigh of relief, and the

small frightened feathered one came out of its
trance and flew away.

"Goodness," I exclaimed impulsively, "what a
shot!" His eyes slid over me, unwinking as an
Indian's.

"Everyone shoots out here," he explained in
crisp, pleasant tones, then lapsed into silence
again.

"These are everyday incidents," said Mollie
casually, her voice as sweet as pie again and ignoring the snubbing she had recently given me.
Then she added, "Don't step on the grasshoppers
—they're so messy."

Thus peace between us was restored. One good
quality I can claim for us Garretts is the equal
speed with which we can turn on and off our
lively tempers, honestly come by through our de-
lightful but extremely mettlesome father.

Our arrival at the next ranch was punctuated
unpleasantly by the shrill squealing of hogs being
slaughtered, so that the tin cup of lukewarm milk
tended me by a young woman with an old, weather-
beaten face, sat uneasily on my stomach. To
Mollie, apparently, it was just another of these
incidents. I glanced at her furtively. Mollie's
sensitive, musical nerves used to go jittery at a
discord struck on the piano or guitar. This country had certainly changed her.

Our sharpshooting friend had disappeared, but
we finally found him back in the coach, rolling a
cigarette.

Every few miles the old bus stopped at some

shed or corral to have the wheels jacked up or to change horses, and it was later in the day, during one of these intervals, that we picked up two more passengers—cowboys. One of them, affecting unbecoming scups, put his foot on the wheel and in a single reach of his long legs landed on the seat beside the driver. The other, with feline agility, sprang into the coach, slumped heavily on an oozing cushion, and spat out a wad of tobacco. These newcomers were rough-looking and uncouth. They wore giddy plaid shirts, and a couple of revolvers pended from their belts.

The sight of them ruffled me. I surveyed the one sitting opposite me uneasily, and my mind drifted back to my last night on the train, when I first heard of Doc Wilson, and suddenly a thrill of apprehension shot through me, and I could feel the blood recede slightly from my face. What could we, two unprotected women alone on these desolate plains, do if our boorish passengers turned out to be bandits? True, the driver, Mollie, and our friendly cowboy were armed, but suppose a gang should unexpectedly join these desperadoes? The sun was disappearing in a savage, fiery sunset, and already its warmth was being withdrawn from these lonely spaces. I shivered and stole closer to Mollie. Sounds travel far in the acute stillness of the plains, and soon I heard a slight padding noise in the rear of us, which increased in volume, coming nearer and nearer, until the tobacco-chewing cowboy whipped out his gun and from the window, with deadly accuracy of aim,

shot an enterprising coyote that had left the pack
to follow us and lope along beside the coach. At
sound of the shot our friendly cowboy glanced up
quickly, and his hand slid to his own revolver like
lightning, but, seeing the mere body of a small
wolf writhing on the prairie, he relaxed his hand
and settled back against the oozing cushions again
and rolled a couple of cigarettes. One of these he
tossed to the coyote killer sitting several feet away,
who caught it in one hairy paw and flipped back
a plug of chewing tobacco with the other.

I primed myself for some illuminating conversation.

"Good hog country," observed the nice cowboy,
pitching back the weed untouched.

"Yeah," rumbled the killer—pause—"you a hog
man?"

"Nope," another silence, then, "are you?"

"Nope." And not another syllable passed between them.

This certainly surprised me. Evidently these
Western stage riders were none too sociable as
compared with the friendliness of the train trav-
elers, but perhaps this tongue-checking gesture
was a frontier convention. So we jogged along,
and from time to time the bulging eyes of the
coyote killer kept straying toward Mollie and me,
and my uneasiness, like a scotched snake, began
to raise its head again. The nice cowboy slept
fitfully.

Silence fell, broken only by the twilight sound
of the wild things. The wind moaned among the

grasses, and we were glad to steal under the worn lap robes provided by the stage. The killer cowboy wrangled off another quid of tobacco and chewed, while Mollie and I whispered together as the old conveyance careened on its uneven way.

Short shafts of dying sunlight mingled with the deepening grey, lavendering the horizon, and all nature seemed to hush as though waiting to welcome the night. I sighed and relaxed a bit, thankful that we had not yet been robbed nor scalped, and my mind was just beginning to lull itself into a sense of security when the stage rolled to a stop before a few sprawling buildings. Here our nice cowboy turned to Mollie and me.

"I'm getting off here," he remarked casually. "The nights are cold, so I am leaving my extra robes for you. The driver will drop them off for me in a day or two."

My heart turned over in panic. Now there would be only the driver to count upon for protection, and night was practically here.

But Mollie was speaking. "Thank you," she replied, "but we won't need them. We will spend the night here."

He shot a swift glance at her.

"Here?" he echoed. "Oh, no, you won't."

We stared at him spellbound for a moment. Finally Mollie drew herself up, measured him haughtily from head to foot, then got out of the coach without another word.

Meanwhile he had picked up the robes, carried them to a fence, where a rangy horse was tied, evidently awaiting him, slapped them across the animal's flanks, loosened the halter, and swung himself into the saddle. The beast plunged straight into the air twice, then, with astonishing rapidity, vanished with its rider into the purple twilight, leaving me oddly depressed yet intrigued.

Our unwelcome passengers bolted from the stage the minute it stopped and shambled stiff legged into the shack that bore the name of "One Eye Jim's." Bewildered and on edge, I clambered out of the diligence and followed Mollie, who was walking boldly toward that identical tavern, there being no other. I glanced about uneasily, for in this particular spot not even sagebrush broke the monotony of the prairie, and the mournful croaking of frogs in slimy, shallow ponds did things to my nerves. Inside the shack, however, it was different. Here smoke swirled in stale, blue wreaths, and the flickering light of tallow candles and blurred chimneys of kerosene lamps disclosed a roomful of cow-smelling men, and a few so-called friendly Indians ranged at a crowded bar or seated at alcohol-stained wooden tables. Circling among them appeared several youngish-looking women with hard, calculating eyes. One of them, dressed in a low-cut green dress, approached us appraisingly.

"Wher-re you goin'?" she queried with veiled insolence, rolling double-barreled r's.

"To Fort Lincoln," replied Mollie coolly.

The woman raised her eyebrows, and her manner changed.

"Oh, you're Government dames, eh?" Then ingratiatingly, "Sure—I knowed it. Can I get you a snack of somethin'?"

"We would like a cup of coffee and a sandwich," returned Mollie, still coolly.

"Right away, dearie—leave it to me," and she was gone.

"This One Eye Jim's wife seems to be kindly disposed," I commented.

"Wife," echoed Mollie scornfully. "She's nobody's wife—just one of—of those women."

"But," I contended innocently, "she's not wearing scarlet."

At this Mollie laughed a bit, but not too loud, for in a place like this it would be wiser to remain inconspicuous, especially with only our driver to defend us. He, by the way, was sunk behind a stack of griddlecakes that would have fed a regiment, which he was gorging with the aid of a huge plate of sausages and a sizable pot of coffee. Of course, it was cold driving—and this made me ask quickly, "Are we going to stay here for the night?"

An excited giggle gave us pause for a moment, and, glancing toward the stairs, we saw one of the women of the place racing up them, pursued by a bearded giant. She permitted herself to be caught, and he snatched her into his gorilla arms and kissed her fiercely.

Mollie was silent for a moment, then murmured, "I think we'll go on."

"After all, the nice cowboy was right," I reflected aloud. "He knew what kind of a place this was," and, unconsciously, my eyes roamed about

for our other passengers. I found them at the
bar, gulping down glass after glass of raw whiskey, and again my fears stirred. Here a slatternly
Chinese slopped up to us, bearing a cracked tray
containing coffee and sandwiches, with a pickle
or two thrown in. These he placed on a dirty table
beside the stove, and after a while, with the inner
man fortified, I told the story of Doc Wilson and
his gang, voicing my fears of the two cowboys.

"Why," said Mollie scornfully, "having held up
the coach only yesterday, they are miles away by
now."

Her logic comforted me somewhat, but not entirely, particularly as I saw our former passengers join the driver, who had polished up his
sundry platters and was preparing to leave. Mollie
and I had been more or less concealed behind the
big stove, and, as we emerged, a number of the
habitués of the establishment saw us for the first
time.

They gaped at us boldly for a moment or two,
then one or two came toward us slowly, but here
the woman in the green dress called to them sharply
and, looking toward us, said something. They immediately fell back and permitted us to pass,
which we did with chins held high.

The driver was waiting beside the stage, and,
sure enough, there were our former passengers,
evidently continuing their trip.

The curiosity I had been stemming now burst
forth.

"That was a nice cowboy who offered us his

buffalo robes," I began, "and—and he rode so beautifully."

The driver nodded, and his mustache waggled.

"He's trim, and neat-looking," I commented, "so different from—from others."

Again the head and mustache jerked affirmatively.

"Friend of yours?"

"Huh?"

"I asked if he was a friend of yours."

He chewed on a toothpick. "Everybody's friends out in these parts, 'ceptin' maybe a few Indians."

"For goodness' sake, come on," cried Mollie impatiently and started to get in the coach.

But my curiosity was by no means appeased. In this sparsely populated country people were reasonably likely to meet again, and who knew but that sometime, perhaps alone and untrammeled by Mollie's remarks, I might encounter once more this knight of the plains? Then I could thank him properly and with maidenly modesty for his courtesy toward two strange women, and mentally I applauded my gracious impulse. Of course, his good looks, superb marksmanship, and horsemanship were not responsible in the least for the birth of my idea, I assured myself demurely, and remarked casually, "He looks prosperous."

"Yeah."

"I suppose he owns a big cattle ranch around here, this Mr.—er—Mr.——" I paused and cleared my throat.

This time my angling brought results. The

driver spat out his toothpick, and his reply rang out like a pistol shot.

"He ain't got no ranch—and his name's Doc Wilson."

Doc Wilson—that name electrified us all to rigid, bewildered attention.

Both the tobacco-chewing cowboy and his partner with the unbecoming scups whirled on the driver.

"Whatcha mean, Doc Wilson?" snarled the former. "He's got a black beard. I seen his picture everywhere with five thousand dollars' reward for him."

"Sure, he's got a beard," reiterated the other cowboy.

"Sure he has," snorted the driver, "but it's false."

Mollie stood as rigid as a ramrod, and if it hadn't been so cold I know I would have fainted. This well-built, well-mannered man a bandit—that statement didn't seem to add up right, yet there was his evasiveness, his reluctance to be drawn into conversation, and I glanced almost apologetically at the other two men. How I had jumped at conclusions and suspected them because of their carelessness in manners and dress!

"Mahogany Christ!" exploded the tobacco chewer, "Why in Hell didn't you tell us?"

"Yeah, why not," mourned the scup wearer, "with a price on his head?"

" 'Cause," retorted the driver, sullen-like, "I want to keep my own head on my shoulders. I seen what happened to others who fooled with Doc Wilson, and," doggedly, "I ain't tellin' nothin'— ransom or no ransom. Besides, he's funny. He ain't vicious when there's women and children about—never touches nothin' then."

"Women and children," I kept repeating to myself. After all, Doc Wilson was a sort of Robin Hood.

Here Mollie came to life.

"What did I tell you," she argued triumphantly. "Just show me anyone who wears snuffy brown, and there'll prove to be something wrong with him or her every time."

"What's that, ma'am?" queried the tobacco chewer.

"Nothing," replied Mollie, tartly. "Let's get started." And we all piled into the stage again, our appetites appeased and resigned to any adventure.

Once more we were reeling in and out of mudholes, the curtains of the old bus jigging in the breeze, as Mollie and I snuggled close under the lap robes. We were too stunned to brand the driver as either coward or self-protector, but Mollie's curiosity was aroused, and she addressed the plaid-shirted one.

"And you," she asked. "Where are you bound?"

"Oh, we're new cowpunchers, ma'am, headed for the Circle A Ranch near here."

So that was settled, but the conversation continued. What about? I hardly knew because my mind was a thousand miles away, but I did catch snatches about his ma "having died at the birth

of his ninth brother" and Pa having "a fierce time
rearing us."

However, I settled back against the cushions
and permitted my thought to drift. The sky was
wide and a million miles high. A star shone, then
another, until the heavens were full of them, and
my imagination traveled back to Doc Wilson. He
was so different from the uncouth rangers of the
plains that I could not help but wonder as to his
background. I sighed as the moon stole out, drench-
ing the night with a white and dewy luster. So
intense a stillness pervaded the plains that we
could hear the panting of a few remaining coyotes
that tagged along in the rear. Then, from far off,
we heard the faint baying of dogs. I roused myself
and remarked to the tobacco-chewing cowboy,
"We must be near a town."

"No, ma'am," he corrected, "that comes from
an Indian village far away."

Indian village—Indians, silent, mysterious, and
again as in the train a finger seemed to reach out
and touch my heart, lightly as a feather, but leaving a shadow. What nonsense, I chided myself.
Why should I permit the presence of a platinum
moon, spraying ghostly light upon the soughing
grasses of the prairies, to play upon my nerves
when I passed hundreds of these villages during
the day with equanimity?

I glanced at Mollie, who, lying against the cushions, had closed her eyes for a moment. Mollie in
the black frock she was wearing for our father. A
deep sigh lifted my breast. Why? I know not.

I turned quickly to the cowpuncher and engaged him in low-toned conversation. Somehow it didn't seem strange, out there, to talk to a total stranger, now that all fear of him had been removed, and, in spite of his whiskey guzzling, he was cold sober. Besides, I wanted to atone in a measure for my unjust suspicions, and there was such a childish simplicity about him. Then, too, the very vastness of the prairies tended to draw human beings together, irrespective of creed or education.

A low, rambling ranch house sprawled before us, and a couple of lighted candles in the window gave an air of hominess.

"Me and Ez gets off here," announced my companion, "and maybe sometime you'll stop by fer some buttermilk. The Circle A's famous for it," he invited, as though the distance between there and Fort Lincoln was a mere stroll.

As we drew up to the place a vicious-looking mastiff, as big as a Shetland pony, came bounding toward us, barking hoarsely. Mollie and I shrank back into the coach, but, at command of the driver, "Down, Jock," the beast subsided as mildly as a calf and contented himself by prowling around us. The driver clambered down from his perch and came to the window.

"Hercules, here," he said, jerking his thumb toward one of the horses, "he's gone lame on me, and we can't go no further tonight."

Meanwhile our cowpunchers had evaporated.

As Mollie and I got out of the stage, the dog approached us and sniffed at us investigatingly, but another peremptory, "Hey, Jock," from the driver quenched his vagrant curiosity, and he padded quietly after us into the house.

So we lodged there that night and were only too glad to occupy a big room in one of the wings. It had a stove, unlighted, in the center of the floor, and in a corner was a high, double bed, minus a leg, which had been propped up with piles of ancient newspapers. An evasive mustiness and the penetrating chill of a place long closed made us rush to the window for air, but the old frame held like a vise, and, tug as we might, we couldn't budge it more than a crack. Too tired for further effort, we decided to lock the door and go to bed. Here, however, we struck a snag, for the latch was broken. Furthermore, there wasn't a chair in the room to use for barricading purposes. What was to be done? We mulled over the question for a few minutes, then, too utterly fagged out to bother about it, we partially undressed and turned in on a thin, straw mattress and pulled over us the sparse threadbare covering. Immediately we fell into an exhausted sleep. I don't know at what hour I awoke and found myself sitting bolt up in bed, listening, every sense keenly alert. Mollie was lying beside me, but she too must have been disturbed, because she was turning restlessly in her sleep. And then I heard it, a deep sigh emanating from beneath the bed. I caught my breath and experienced the queerest sensation of my life, for the mattress began to rise and fall. Cold chills frolicked up and down my spine.

Mollie was now awake, and I leaned over her, whispering cautiously, "Don't move. Someone is in this room. Listen." We did, tensely, and, after what seemed an interminable period, the mattress heaved again, and again came that deep-drawn sigh. We clutched each other, and Mollie pulled my sleeve. I leaned close to her.

"You're on the outside," she whispered, "and my revolver, loaded, is on that far table. Can you make it?"

Could I make it? She expected me to leap out of bed and have my feet grabbed. Not on her nor my life would I do such a thing. Yet I did just that, after the next heaving episode took place. I took a flying leap into the center of the room and, rushing to the table, fumbled about for the pistol, which Mollie must have shoved carelessly among some papers and magazines scattered on top. Where was it? Where was it?

My trembling fingers simply couldn't locate it, but they did contact a box of matches. I grabbed them eagerly and struck a light, and, by the flare, I saw a big head and shoulders emerging from under the bed. I was so stunned that I stood there dumbly. I couldn't scream. I just waited, and then a cold nose touched me, sniffed, and, yawning expansively, the mastiff turned away and sought the foot of the bed, where he plopped himself on the floor heavily. Evidently he had crept into the room through the unlocked door and had contemplated a restful night, which we had selfishly disturbed. Suddenly I realized that it was bitter cold and that I was shivering. I cautiously approached the bed so as not to arouse unduly our self-appointed protector, slipped in, and planted my freezing feet in the middle of Mollie's back. She protested loudly, and the mastiff growled, and, after a bit, she began to chuckle softly.

"Isn't it the beatenest thing," she whispered, using the vernacular of Mammy Lindy, "this beast that frightened the life out of us is taking care of us."

"Taking care of us," I echoed sleepily. "On the contrary, I think we have usurped his bedroom, and he is just tolerating us."

When a rap on the half-open door aroused us, the sun was shining into the room and our hairy host had vanished. I rolled out of bed and made for the washstand, where I broke a film of ice in the pitcher and poured some water into a tin basin.

"Get up, Mollie," I kept calling. "It must be late." But, encased in a cocoon of bedding, she paid no attention.

My ablutions were sketchy, and my fingers were so cold that I could scarcely button my gown, but I cried exasperatedly, "Do you want to be left behind? Get up and wash."

Slowly the cocoon unfurled itself, and, sitting up in bed, Mollie thrust out one small bare foot experimentally.

"I'll get up," she conceded grudgingly, "but I'll be darned if I'll wash."

This, coming from my immaculate sister, tickled my risibles, and I giggled.

Well, we finally attained the long breakfast table, along with shirt-sleeved cowpunchers, who swallowed their knives and gobbled their food like hungry dogs, but their eyes were as clear and honest as that beautiful day. So we partook of muddy coffee and ham and eggs floating in grease, then got under way for our last lap until we struck the railroad. The ride was practically a duplicate of that of the day before, but as we approached Grand Rapids, Dakota, the wagon trails improved a bit so that we made better time.

When we finally arrived and climbed aboard the train we felt as though we had reached heaven. Of course, we waited on the usual hot boxes, eating shacks, and enthusiastic hunters, but these annoyances we bore with fortitude.

The monotonous rocking of the train, the endless, endless prairies, the spanless turquoise sky, served, somewhat, as soporifics, yet, as from under half-closed eyes I watched the immense spaces glide by, my drowsing imagination was jolted to wakefulness from time to time by sudden miniature dramas. For instance, I glimpsed, sepulchred among the tall grasses, the brown and white body of a dead calf, over which hovered a flock of hungry buzzards which were voraciously picking the tender bones clear of all flesh. In contrast, farther on, I saw in the distance a herd of bisons nibbling in bovine contentment at the inviting green succulence of early spring, yet, a mile beyond, my attention was abruptly focused upon a huge, black hulk, sprawled beside a cedar bush. Here, two copper-colored Indians, half-nude, were bending above it and with swift, sharp knives were carving from the buffalo carcass, hunks of raw meat, which they were devouring ravenously.

This set me to musing upon the eternal cycle of life and evolution, beginning with budding seedlings that nourish and pad with solid flesh the feathered creatures and herbivorous animals, upon which, in turn, birds of prey and carnivorous beasts, and finally, man, of vegetarian and meat appetites, the most destructive of them all, for he kills, not only for food, but to satisfy the vanity of beautiful women, who wrap their graces in the gorgeous pelts of many harmless and inoffensive wild creatures of plain and jungle.

At Fargo, Mollie wired Donald when we would arrive in Bismarck, and, from that time on, we had nothing to do but watch the poker players, peek through field glasses at the herds of animals and Indians, almost constantly passing, eat, and sleep.

The train, only three hours late, pulled into Bismarck about five o'clock in the afternoon on the second day of our trip. I glued my nose to the window, expecting to see the surging crowds that weaved in and out of the depots at Washington or Chicago, but the crude wooden station was almost empty, except for a few cowboys, ranchmen, and some railroad hands.

Suddenly, from behind a wooden pillar, stepped the tall, lithe figure of an army officer in uniform, wearing a forage cap which bore the number 7,

Lieutenant Donald McIntosh, killed at the Battle of the Little
Bighorn.

Colonel Samuel D. Sturgis, Seventh Cavalry. (He was addressed by his Civil War title of General.)

and a pair of shoulder straps showing the insignia of a first lieutenant.

"There's Donald," exclaimed Mollie as excitedly as though they had been separated a month.

He hurried towards us, and, as I looked into his strong, purposeful face and kindly, dark eyes, I suddenly knew that Mollie was a very lucky woman.

At a sign from him a soldier, whom I hadn't seen, collected our luggage and carried it out to the street, where a funny old rig transported us across town toward the river.

Mollie was all agog for army news. Had Mrs. Custer returned from St. Paul, and how did she look? Had the Inspector arrived? When would the regiment go into camp? Were the troops coming from Fort Rice?

Donald smiled, and snow-white teeth flashed from behind his thin lips.

"The Inspector arrived this afternoon," he informed us, "and Custer is staging a full-dress, mounted parade in his honor tomorrow. Mrs. Custer has returned and looks well. Date of camp making is not decided, but the troops from Rice will join us."

Mollie beamed.

"What fun," she said cheerily. "We haven't seen the rest of the regiment for months."

Donald turned to me and remarked, "Of course, all this is Greek to you, but we are about to start on a sixty-day campaign to penetrate the unknown interior of the Black Hills. This is the heart of the Sioux country, and, in order to maintain a controlling influence over the tribe, General Sheridan recommends the establishment of a large cavalry post somewhere in or around this location, and it is our job to look over the ground."

"Oh," I exclaimed impulsively, "can't Mollie and I go?"

He shook his head. "I'm afraid not. It's too— er—uncertain."

"Yes," amended Mollie, "but there are plenty of things that would be certain. You would be literally biting the alkali dust. You'd be living on canned meat, if the game should be scarce. The coyotes would make night hideous for you, and you'd run into lots of rattlers."

The picture was not alluring, so I allowed my gaze to drift along the main street of Bismarck. It was unpaved and presented a huge, mud bog, through which horses strained and men in high leather boots tramped up to their ankles. The low frame houses, weather stained, consisted mostly of fodder stores, saloons, and laundries where moon-faced Celestials plied their trade. Cowboys, resplendent in chaps, wide-brimmed hats, and flashy neckerchiefs, swarmed all over the place, splashing on pedestrians the mud flung from the squashing hoofs of their restless horses. Stony-faced Indians, wearing a single, vivid feather in their hair and wrapped in multicolored blankets, sat astride their ponies, which picked their way daintily through the muck. Wide-shouldered, bearded ranchmen strode beside oxcarts and flipped the lash of their long, rawhide whips above the backs of the patient beasts when they stalled in the mire. I had read of such scenes, but only stark reality could depict their primitive, though picturesque, settings.

Vaguely I heard the droning voices of Mollie and Donald, but now I was recalled to myself abruptly.

"Well, here's where we take the boat," announced my brother-in-law, and the rig stopped before the wharf.

"Boat?" I echoed.

"Of course," said Mollie, "because the old bridge is being repaired."

The soldier jumped down from his seat beside the driver and was stowing the luggage into a wide, flat boat. Several stubby-bearded men in rough clothing, and having bony, powerful hands, sat at the oars. The sun was dipping toward the horizon, and muddy waters were lapping the wharf. A flutter of malaise prompted my question.

"Er—how long will it take to cross?"

"Oh, 'bout an hour," answered one of the rowers. "That is, if the river don't rise no higher."

The turbulent Missouri was racing along sullenly, and I glanced toward Mollie, who was laughing about something with Donald, and I envied her nonchalance. I swallowed hard and clung tensely to the boat side.

By the grace of God, and strong arms, and quick eyes on the lookout for drifting logs, or the occasional body of a horse, cow, cat, or dog, suddenly engulfed by the river in its recent rampage, we reached the other shore in safety.

And here I caught my first glimpse of an army ambulance, with which method of travel I was to become intimately acquainted for many years. High and cumbersome, it resembled somewhat the coach we had left a few days before, but it was drawn by four mules and driven by a soldier. A carbine lay beside him, and around his waist was buckled a cartridge belt. Under the front axle of the ambulance was a bucket suspended for the feeding or watering of the mules, and under the rear one hung a water keg. Our first soldier, who turned out to be Lieutenant McIntosh's striker, transferred our luggage from the boat to the ambulance boot, a sort of large trunk space at the back. After that he climbed to a seat beside the driver, and we got into the ambulance and started for Fort Lincoln, some four miles distant, through the clogging gumbo mud.

We bumped along slowly, detouring where the freshets still made traveling difficult, and the night came on. Again the wild things crept under cover as though hiding from the crescent moon, which blazed as a great white diamond embedded in a dark background of star gems, vying with each other in color from Martian rubies, ambers, lavenders to the exquisite aqua blues of Venus and Sirius. Under this canopy of glory a few belated covered wagons struggled on toward Bismarck, also Indians, alone or in pairs, and as silent as the night, passed us either going to town or coming from it, and always they turned and gazed after us enigmatically.

What an unconscionable time it took us to travel those few miles! But finally flickering lights in the distance heralded the outposts of the garrison.

First Days at Fort Lincoln

iii

FORT LINCOLN, built for cavalry occupancy, was located in a valley flanked by bluffs on the top of which was an infantry post.

As we approached the reservation, soldier sentinels, clutching carbines, blocked our path with the sharp challenge, "Who goes there?" However, recognizing Lieutenant McIntosh, they brought their guns to a thudding rest, saluted stiffly, and permitted us to pass. Standing at motionless attention and silhouetted against the lunar light that flooded those seemingly limitless prairies, the alert guardianship of those silent soldiers gave me the thrill of a stage drama.

At last we were rumbling down Officers' Row, and just as we stopped before my brother-in-law's quarters, the clear notes of a bugle came drifting across the parade ground. Taps, the most beautiful call in all the service, was sounding. It roused in me conflicting emotions. Its elusive sadness combined with its promise of rest—rest that was sometimes merely protective, as now when one by one the lights of the barracks went out, assuring the tired soldier of a safely guarded sleep—and then the other, the eternal rest, the reward of lasting peace.

Muscle bound, we got stiffly out of the ambu-

lance. The striker leaped to the ground and retrieved our luggage from the boot. A ray of light
from the open door beckoned to us, and a bland
smile, radiating from a round, ebony face, welcomed us.

"Iwilla," said Mollie, addressing her cook, "this
is my sister, Miss Katie Garrett."

I had heard many odd names given to the dusky
race, but this one capped them all.

"Oh," I exclaimed, suddenly homesick for my
own blessed Mammy. "Oh—er—Iwilla?" I paused
questioningly.

"Yas'um. Dey calls me Iwilla fer short, but I
was christened 'I Will Arise,'" and a red-
bandannaed head bowed respectfully.

I controlled my impulse to laugh, then resumed,
"I'm glad you're here. Iwilla. I won't be lonesome
now. Mrs. McIntosh must have told you about our
dear Mammy back home, who nursed us all from
birth."

Iwilla chuckled. "She sure has, Miss Katie,
and you-all must be powerful cold an' hungry, but
I'se got supper fer you," and she waddled off,
leaving me to look around the McIntosh home.

It was a detached frame house, accommodating
two families, evidently hastily constructed, as the
wind blew through unseen crevices and rattled
the windows. It was lighted by kerosene lamps
and candles, and the walls of the medium-sized
living room were hung with old canvas tenting
to make the place warmer. A lighted stove in the
middle of the room threw out welcome heat. A

few campstools and unpainted chairs were scattered around, and a fur rug or two served as floor coverings.

The only piece of furniture that lifted this atmosphere of dreariness was a piano that Mollie had shipped from St. Paul. If marooned even in the Sahara Desert, music in some form she would have. On top of the instrument sprawled a Martin guitar, a banjo, and a violin. The dining room beyond displayed another stove and a table made of three wooden planks stretched across two carpenter's horses. This type of table served several purposes in those old army days, such as a bed, an ironing board, and a bench. More campstools, more fur rugs, and extra chairs completed the sumptuous furnishings.

I glanced at Mollie, who had been brought up on family antique mahogany and rosewood and had studied her lessons at a table sacred to the card games of General Washington when he used to visit our ancestors, but she was smiling happily as she explained, "It's no use buying anything worth while until we settle down."

"Of course," I agreed, still unable to understand her complete contentment, and resolved that nothing would ever induce me to abandon the comforts of the East.

Just then Donald came in, but not alone, for I heard a jolly voice saying, "Nonsense, Tosh, no one is ever tired out here," and a dapper little officer brushed past.

Mollie flashed a swift smile at him as she said

Lieutenant Benjamin H. Hodgson, killed at the Battle of the Little Bighorn.

Captain Myles Moylan.

banteringly, "Good heavens, Benny, can't you ever keep out of this house?" Then, to me, "Katie, this is Mr. Hodgson." Socially, a lieutenant is always addressed as Mr.

"Yes," continued Donald, winking at me, "he's always around at feeding time."

Lieutenant Hodgson grinned, then, coming forward, took both my hands in his—he was so young and boyish.

"Don't pay any attention to their rudeness, Miss Katie," he counseled with mock gravity. "They just can't help it, but I couldn't resist the temptation of being the first to welcome you."

"Don't let him fool you, Katie," admonished Mollie, teasingly. "He adores Iwilla's cooking."

"Rise" had just entered with a steaming steak and fried potatoes, the striker following with griddle cakes.

"It's a base slander," defended Benny, drawing up chairs to the board. "Besides, I loathe Iwilla's griddle cakes, don't I, Iwilla?"

"Rise" chuckled and returned to the kitchen for coffee.

"Miss Katie, do you shoot?" asked our uninvited guest. I shook my head and imagined that his face fell.

"Ride?" hopefully.

"No," I was forced to admit.

"Too bad," he opined, "but—er—we'll change all that."

Well, we had the jolliest sort of meal, then Lieutenant Hodgson left, saying as he did so,

"Good night, Miss Katie. Maybe I'll be over for breakfast."

"Try it, and you'll be thrown out," warned Donald, grinning.

"Yes, I know," retorted Benny, throwing his arm across the latter's shoulder, "but I'll risk it."

And he was gone, that merry boy, who in the spring of 1876 withdrew his resignation from the army for the fun of just one last campaign. It was his last, poor Benny. Yet there are those who do not believe in destiny.

Upstairs I found my room devoid of every comfort. It contained bare necessities only. A grey government blanket did rug service. Another, marked in big black letters, U.S.A., covered the soldier's cot. A campstool, table, and dressing table, consisting of shelves nailed into a packing box and turned on its side, a tin pitcher, a basin, and a crude mirror completed the furnishings. However, being dead tired, I slipped gratefully in between unbleached cotton sheets and immediately fell into a deep sleep.

Suddenly, at dawn, I was awakened by the sound of a rapid bugle call, followed by the noise of cannon. Half asleep, bewildered, I sat for a moment in bed trembling. Indians, I decided. They must be attacking. Jumping out of the cot, I ran to Mollie's room and banged on the door.

"Who is it?" called the drowsy voice of my brother-in-law.

"It's Katie," I panted. "Let me in."

"What's the matter?" asked Mollie sleepily.

"Don't you hear the firing and bugle call?" I cried impatiently. "The Indians are coming."

Then I caught the sound of Mollie's chuckle as Donald explained.

"Just the reveille gun. Go on back to bed."

Feeling very small and ignorant, I crawled into the cot again, and only awoke at the first call for guard mounting. When I opened my eyes they fell upon the beaming face of Iwilla, who was standing looking down at me and carrying a tray of ham and eggs, hot biscuit, and a pot of coffee.

"Mornin', Miss Katie," she grinned. "Miss McIntosh say you is to rest an' eat your breakfast calm liko."

She placed her appetizing burden on a small, unpainted table and set the whole beside me.

"Shall I pour your coffee, Honey?" she asked, seeing me rub my eyes.

"Please do, Iwilla," I replied, and took a whiff of the Santos brand, the only kind the army carried at that time.

" 'Pears like you-all ain't been feelin' so perky," she continued.

"Oh," I laughed, "you're thinking of my cough. That disappeared long ago," and I bit into a biscuit, as hungry as a hunter.

"I'se powerful glad to hear it, 'cause Lieutenant and Miss McIntosh dey jest worriet theirselves to death 'bout you. When you needs hot water, jess give me a hoo-hoo, an' I'll bring it right up."

I hopped out of bed, dragged the table over to the window, and, while eating, my eyes swept the parade ground where I had my first view of guard mounting. It intrigued me, even though I didn't understand it, and I loved the band.

Later I learned why each soldier and his equipment was so carefully scrutinized at this morning inspection. The man with the most military bearing and tidiness captured the reward of being orderly for the day, escaping the monotony of military duty, drills, and tending stables.

The fresh air penetrated my nostrils and made me ambitious to get into my clothes, especially as I heard Mollie on the porch gaily greeting the passers-by, so obediently I "hoo-hooed" for my hot water, splashed around in it a bit, then jumped into my frock and hurried downstairs.

An officer with a sandy mustache came springing along the board walk.

"Good morning, Mrs. McIntosh," he saluted Mollie, and started to pass on, but she hailed him.

"Not so fast, Captain Moylan. I want you to meet my little sister."

"I'm in an awful rush," he protested, "but I'm glad to meet you, Miss Garrett. You see, we knew your name before we knew you," and he reached out and gave my hand a warm squeeze. "How are you?"

"Feeling refreshed from a good night's rest and plenty of ozone," I replied pertly.

"Good. Do you shoot?"

I shook my head.

"Ride?"

Again I fell short.

"Oh," a pause, then worriedly to Mollie, "got any ice?"

"No—what for?"

"Little Donohue."

"What, again?" ejaculated Mollie sympathetically. He nodded, and I looked askance from one to the other.

"Who is little Donohue?" I inquired.

"The best saddler in the regiment," explained Captain Moylan, "but he will get soused every payday, and we've got to ice him out of it."

My face must have registered a complete blank, because he laughed heartily.

"You see," he continued, "when a man is absolutely out, the quickest way to sober him is to rub a piece of ice up and down his spine. Works like a charm. Well, good-by."

The next officer I met was lean, genial Lieutenant Wallace, with his fair hair, long neck, and general appearance of attenuation.

"Glad to meet you, Miss Katie," he said. "Do you shoot?"

"No," I quavered, beginning to be ashamed of my deficiencies.

"Ride?"

I shook my head guiltily.

"Too bad," and, lifting his cap, he, too, was gone.

I pondered a moment, then added somewhat irrelevantly, "But he's nice."

"Of course, he's nice. They're all nice," retorted Mollie with finality and opening her eyes with surprise.

And so they seemed. Sometimes I wonder if it was the lack of fuss and pretensions, with everyone knowing the pay of the other fellow, that made the army in general so united, but it was more than that. There was also the very solitude of their mutual existence—just a handful of people, so to speak, afloat upon an uncharted sea of desolation, miles and miles from civilization—and the shared hardships of a bleak climate with its privations, and the daily perils they faced together. These were the factors that brought these army pioneers closer to each other in some instances than many brothers and sisters, and forged ties of friendship that neither time nor circumstances could sever.

My sister was the type essentially suited for army life, physically strong, fearless, jolly, witty. Her music was a godsend in that wilderness, and, above all, she and Donald adored each other. Their home, whether in tent or quarters, was a mecca for young people, and often in the quiet night after tattoo we would all gather around her, and she and I would sing and play on our guitars—for I had brought mine along—while the others joined in the chorus.

Donald, quiet of voice and manner, had nevertheless a keen sense of humor and was one of the most beloved officers of the regiment. He combined the brilliant mind of a student with a marked flair for military science, and to his friends he was affectionaly known as "Tosh." Personally, I loved him as my own brother.

But to return to the morning of my first guard mounting. Scarcely had Lieutenant Wallace left, when along came Lieutenant Hodgson, and I flashed a smile at him, expecting him to join us, but he didn't. On the contrary, his laughing mouth was set in a tight line of preoccupation, and, merely lifting his cap, he passed on with that rapid, measured step that always proclaims the West Pointer.

"What's the matter with him?" I gasped, a bit hurt.

"Nothing," answered Mollie. "He's just busy."

And then I began to learn something of the dual personality of Uncle Sam's soldiers. Off duty they relax with the abandon of boys out of school, but, on duty, they snap into grim-visaged, purposeful men.

Donald came along in company with some other young officers—Lieutenants Hare, Nave, McDougall, and Captain French—but they, too, were preoccupied and, beyond acknowledging Mollie's introduction, paid me scant attention and hurried on.

Mollie followed Donald into the house, leaving me chair-rocking on the porch. Along the board walk strolled two women, both young and hatless, and the cut of their out-of-date gowns betrayed a long absence from civilization. One was slightly plump, with blue eyes and masses of fair hair, the other as dark and slim as a schoolgirl.

Said the fair one, extending her hand, "I am Mrs. Moylan."

"Oh," I exclaimed impulsively, "I met your husband this morning," eagerly, "and did he finally ice little Donohue sober?"

She threw back her head and laughed.

"I don't know—officially," she replied, "but he usually does."

Whereupon, for a moment, the three of us made merry.

"And I am Mrs. Yates," stated the girl with the gorgeous eyes, "and I would know you anywhere as Mrs. McIntosh's sister."

Charlotte Moylan, childless, and one of the most capable women in the regiment, was to become my constant companion in the long years that followed the Custer Massacre, for fate always threw us together in the same garrison, and we naturally had much in common that those who joined the Seventh later could not quite share.

But it was Annie Yates, grave, sweet Annie, wife of Captain Yates, who captured my affection at once. There was something so sincere and compelling in her great dark eyes, a vivacity of youth and fun and a warmth of nature that reached out to everyone. As I look back upon those days, I realize that she was one of the most unusual of them all. Already she had two children, was a splendid housekeeper, could dance like a fairy, yet was one of the best-read and brainiest women I ever knew, and, even after her great tragedy, our close friendship continued down the years that she survived her hero-husband until the hour of her death.

My visitors only remained a short time, running over, they explained, just to get acquainted. After they left I heard the clatter of horses' hoofs dashing along the road, and, glancing up, I saw a mounted officer, followed by a mounted orderly, thundering past. The former challenged my curiosity because he was so distinctive. Tall, almost boyishly slender, he sat his saddle as though born in it. Golden curls, matching the yellow broadcloth stripes which ran down the sides of his blue trousers and were tucked in at the knees into troop boots, tumbled rebelliously from under a wide-brimmed white felt hat, shading keen, blue eyes that moved with a flash rather than a glance about him. A tawny mustache bordered his mouth. The thin, florid face, though not handsome, was singularly arresting, for it glowed with an expression of combined vitality and recklessness. I had seen too many photographs of him not to recognize General George Armstrong Custer—known to his family as Autie.

After lunch Lieutenant McIntosh was plunged in troop matters at the barracks, Mollie was taking a nap, and I had started to scribble a few lines home, but the constant opening and shutting of the front door to admit well-meaning souls put an end to my writing activities. It was difficult to duck these friendly invasions, because the doors of the quarters were left open day and night; thus one's home became a social thoroughfare, more or less, according to one's popularity. I nodded to Iwilla to notify Mollie of this influx of visitors, but "Rise" said in a stage whisper, " 'Tain't no

use, Miss Katie. Eberybody knows dat Miss Mc-
Intosh ain't losin' her nap fer nobody."

So there was nothing to do but get acquainted
without Mollie and feed our genial interlopers
with tea, toasted hardtack—something like pilot
biscuit, yeastless, saltless, tasteless, but a prime
favorite with the army—and tart jelly made from
buffalo berries.

Notwithstanding, we passed a pleasant afternoon and didn't realize the hour until Donald came
springing up the steps to dress for parade. Then
everybody scattered hastily for her own quarters.

By order of General Custer the parade and retreat was to be a full-dress, mounted affair, and
was to be held on the wide, level plain on the outskirts of the garrison, which offered a better range
for the maneuvers than the parade ground proper.
Besides, the General was a showman, it seemed,
and craved an audience for his spectacle. And he
got it—not only from the outlying infantry post,
but curious ranchmen from neighboring ranches
filtered into the reservation, along with Indian
scouts, squaws, and even people from Bismarck.
When Mollie and I arrived in our buckboard, a
huge semicircle of spectators had already been
formed of broncos, Indian ponies and vehicles of
all kinds and sizes, the outlay resembling vaguely
an arena.

As I recall my first impression of that mounted
parade, I realize that it imparted a glamor to my
army life that nothing ever quite equaled. I can
see now those six troops of cavalry, the horses of

which had been selected by experts and groomed to perfection, their glossy skins shining in the sun like cut velvet. Atop these superb creatures sat men like centaurs, their chins held in by the leather understraps of black helmets—or maybe they were of the deepest blue, which appeared black. Anyway, these helmets were decorated by gold spread eagles, and thick yellow plumes floated from gold spikes in the center of the crown. The cavalry uniforms were of blue and gold, and sabers swung at the sides. The officers' equipment was supplemented by kidney-shaped yellow and gold epaulets, bearing the insignia of rank, repeated on the collar. A gold thread saber belt, heavy gold cords and tassels worn across the breast, and broadcloth canary-yellow stripes which ran down the outside of the trousers, the latter encased in regimental high-topped boots, completed the outfit.

But now for the parade itself. Ranking officers down to the first sergeants bawled their orders against the breeze, and on swept the advancing columns with flags and guidons flying. The lines formed or divided, undulating in trots or gallops, according to commands or bugle calls, all of which were understood by the horses. It was amazing to note the almost human precision of the end and center animals as they helped wheel or straighten the line, but it was the regimental adjutant who drew my special attention. This officer, of course, played the most conspicuous part in the whole parade, because he had to combine splendid military bearing and technical training. He was here and there and everywhere. I followed his every movement from his command, "Sound off," to the band, which swung into a spirited march, through to his trots, gallops, halts, drawn saber, his weaving in and out of the lines or between the Colonel and center of the regiment, until he wheeled, saluted the Colonel, and reported, "Sir, the parade is formed."

Here my attention strayed a moment to the Colonel, who with drawn saber was putting the command through snappy saber exercises, concluding with, "Return saber!"

The rhythmic flash of metal in the rays of the setting sun and the soft breeze flicking the golden plumes painted a picture of hundreds of individual yellow flags, and I turned enthusiastically toward Mollie, only to find her promising someone in the next carriage to send a recipe of Iwilla's chokecherry pie, made from a tiny berry so dry and shrunken that nothing but a skin was drawn over a big pit. The taste of it was so bitter and astringent that the mouth was practically closed for half an hour or more after eating. However, it was labeled fruit, and any kind of fresh fruit was a luxury in Dakota.

Disgusted, I settled back in the rig and gave myself up to an orgy of military maneuvers. A line of sergeants in front of the command reported separately that A, B, or C troop was present or accounted for, the adjutant relaying the information to the Colonel. Then he published a long list of orders, and between watching these things and trying to keep track of what was taking place in the ranks at the same time, I was pretty nearly cross-eyed.

There was more pageantry, of course, but some of its high lights intrigued me particularly, such as the little private parade of the band, the breathtaking passing of the troops in review as they swept across the plain, also that moment when the officers wheeled their horses into line, the adjutant galloping from the rear and filling up the space left open for him, and at his command, "Officers, center, march!" the whole line advanced as one man and one horse upon the Colonel and his staff, while the band blared. The subsequent order, "Officers, halt!" and the deft reining of the horses to a sudden stop, the abrupt silence of the band as the officers saluted the Colonel and staff, keeping their hands to their visors until the salute was returned. Then the breaking of the line as they joined their commander and awaited "Retreat"—the most impressive note of the military day. Measured bars of music played by the cornets rang out upon the air, and, as the last note died away, a single cannon salute, known as the sunset gun, reverberated from earth to sky. Simultaneously the Stars and Stripes began to slip from their moorings atop the emergency pole—the flagpole proper being situated inside the garrison. The band played at slow beats the "Star Spangled Banner" while, at the same time, the flag floated gracefully down from its high, sentinel post. Reverent hands reached out to protect it from touching the ground, until it rested safely in the arms of the soldiers detailed to receive it.

The parade was over. The officers, dismissed, were sauntering here and there. The first sergeants drew their sabers, rode in front of their troops, commanded "Post," and, with the band now striking a brisk military air, the column marched off the wide plain.

As horses, necks arched, tails streaming in the breeze, and horsemen in shining helmets disappeared, I drew a tremendous sigh, for it had all been so gorgeous and inspiring that my mind hurdled back many centuries.

Finally Mollie's voice recalled me to the present, asking banteringly, "Well, where have you been?"

"Back to the Middle Ages," I answered dreamily, "with Waverley's gaily attired palfreys, and knights of old carrying halberds, and crusaders with plumed helmets and glittering shields."

She regarded me musingly. "It's a pity you didn't use more of that imagination when I was teaching you the piano," she remarked.

"It's a pity you didn't use more patience with a nervous child," I flashed back.

No offense was intended by either of us, but, as a family, we applied our father's slogan: "Never be mealymouthed—assert yourself."

What retort she might have made was lost in the confusion of breaking up the semicircle of spectators. Indian ponies scampered away, the thumping hoofs of cowboys' rangy animals ploughed up the soil, various rigs of ranchmen squeaked

A group of officers of the Seventh Cavalry.

Lieutenant Charles Braden.

in their leisurely, homeward direction. The rest of us, including the members of the infantry post, sought our own quarters, dinner bound.

Just then an officer rode up beside us and greeted Molly. He was squarely built, square-headed, bearded, had nice dark eyes, and rode a thickset horse.

"Oh, Katie," my sister exclaimed, "I want you to meet Mr. Braden."

We talked a few minutes, and then came the inevitable questions.

"Do you shoot? Do you ride?"

I was becoming sensitive to my military shortcomings, and the conversation lagged. Presently he rode away.

"Good Old Gothic," murmured Mollie, looking after him. "They call him that because he is so solidly built, and so reliable. Last August, while in camp on the Yellowstone, the Indians attacked in large numbers. He, with a small detachment, was charged by a hundred warriors and, with the most wonderful exhibition of cool nerve, maintained his position and repulsed them, although he was shot through the thighbone."

Later on, when I knew him better, I realized what a great soul he was. Though he accepted his wound stoically, it compelled him to retire not long afterward. However, he did not pass the rest of his life in vain regrets for his lost career and high rank which time and lengthened service would have brought him, but, on the banks of the Hudson, he established the Braden Preparatory School for West Point, which still bears his name and is known throughout the nation.

All along the road we were accosted by "knights in shining helmets," until it became bewildering. There were Lieutenants Algernon Smith, Craycroft, and McDougall; Captains Thompson and Ilsley, the latter having a blond goatee, Captain Tom Custer, brother of the General, and the regimental adjutant, Lieutenant Cook. Wearing helmets that reached down to their eyebrows, they looked alike, except for those wearing beards, so I warned them laughingly, "If I don't speak to you the next time I see you, just blame it on the helmets and concealing chin straps." As a matter of fact, Tom Custer always wore his helmet, caps, and campaign hats tilted way over his eyes, and it was only when I had studied the particular slant of his head that I learned to distinguish him from the other fair-haired officers.

"Why do you cover your face so?" I asked him one time.

"It's a disguise," he confided with a perfectly straight face. "You see, they're after me—for killing a Chinaman."

And being entirely dumb, I hugged the awful secret to my bosom for many a long day.

The questions, "Do you ride—shoot?", which got on my nerves, I construed as being a mere cavalry platitude, corresponding somewhat with the question, "How do you like our city?" asked of strangers back East.

The Custers

iv

THAT EVENING after dinner Mollie, Donald, and I wandered over to Custer's quarters, which were somewhat similar to ours, except that they were larger and stood alone. The porch was filled with people, many of whom I had already met.

I shall never forget my first impression of Elizabeth Custer. Slim, girlish looking in a light-colored, out-of-date frock, she had quiet, intelligent eyes that met one with interest rather than criticism. Her skin was soft and smooth, but her face had more than prettiness. Character was written there, and when she smiled she warmed one with her friendliness. The light breeze lifted her wavy dark hair slightly as she turned to greet Mollie and Donald.

"Here she is, Mrs. Custer," announced Mollie, shoving me forward slightly. "My little sister."

I looked up a bit consciously, and, as I encountered the kind eyes of Elizabeth Custer, I knew that I was to love her all my life. She held out her hand to me, smiling and speaking in low, sweet tones.

"So here you are at last, little Miss Katie—we've heard so much about you," she said, covering my hand in both of hers. "Welcome to the army, my dear, and in no time we'll put color in those pale

Eastern cheeks of yours that I noticed at parade."

"You saw me at parade?"

"Yes, indeed, but you were too thrilled by it to be interrupted; wasn't it magnificent?"

"Oh, just marvelous," I replied.

Here a babble of tongues clamored for Mollie and Donald, and they were swept into the house. A moment later I heard Mollie at the piano, swinging into the strains of a waltz, and the place was turned into an impromptu hop, leaving the porch as empty as a gourd.

Suddenly, racketing horses' hoofs tore along the road and stopped in front of the house. A lithe figure sprang to the ground, tied the animal deftly to a wooden newel post, and came striding stiff-leggedly up the walk.

"Oh, Autie," called Mrs. Custer, "you're just in time to meet Mrs. McIntosh's sister, Miss Katie Garrett."

The General was now beside us.

"Isn't she pretty?" persisted Mrs. Custer.

I felt the color dye my face, though the moonlight concealed it as the General shook my hand.

"Of course she is," he agreed gallantly. "But I'm sure the sunlight will do her more justice than the moonlight."

At this we all laughed, which put us at our ease.

"I saw you passing our quarters this morning," I offered eagerly, "and you were riding the most beautiful horse."

His eyes sparkled with boyish pleasure.

"That was Dandy—and he is a dandy."

"Vic is just as fine," contended Mrs. Custer.

"Yes, but—— Come and see Dandy," and cupping my elbow in his hand, he steered me down the steps toward the newel post, which the horse was placidly nibbling.

The General passed his hand caressingly over the horse's glossy neck, and instantly the creature was dipping his nose towards his master's pocket.

"Here, you old humbug!" exclaimed the General, producing a lump of sugar. "Can you see his splendid legs?" he inquired, as proud of his pet as a woman is with an Angora. I peered down obediently and listened to the speech that summed up the good and bad points of a horse.

"You're fond of horses, aren't you?" he asked.

"Oh, yes, indeed."

"I see you have had a lot to do with them."

"Oh, yes, indeed," I echoed.

"That's fine—I've a splendid mount, a little too mettlesome for most women to ride, but I'd like to have you try him."

"I'd love to," I rejoined, lured on by the Devil.

"Then I'll send him over to your quarters tomorrow morning," he promised with finality.

"I'll be waiting for him," I replied, and then, at the very thought of it, my knees began to shake. Why had I done this—why had I played this foolish part? Suddenly I felt my eyes filling with tears, and I was homesick and unhappy, and I wanted my lady-mother.

The General caught my lachrymose countenance in the moonlight and glanced at me in panic.

"Why — why, Miss Katie!" he exclaimed. "What's the matter?"

"Nothing—much," I sniffed. "Only I—I lied. I don't know anything about horses—I'm afraid of 'em—and I can't shoot either—I'm—I'm afraid of firearms, too—and I feel like a fool, not being able to do anything that others do out here."

For a moment he was silent, then seeing that the tears would flow in spite of myself, he jerked a handkerchief from his blouse and gently wiped them away with an expression of gallant concern which comforted me considerably.

"Then why don't you learn?"

"It might be a good idea," I conceded. Then defensively, "But everyone has offered to teach me, and no one has done anything about it."

"Tch-tch," he commiserated, "and you have been here the whole of twenty-four hours. That's a crime. But here's another idea. Suppose Tom and I take you in hand tomorrow morning?"

"Oh, will you?" I ejaculated gratefully. "And you do forgive me?"

He laughed. "As a matter of fact, I should ask your forgiveness."

"Mine?" I asked, startled. "What for?"

"Because I knew all along that you couldn't ride or shoot. Tom and Hodgson—all of them—told me, and I was mean enough to lead you on. I apologize."

So we declared a truce, and had just turned to join the others when the greatest commotion took place. A small buffalo calf loped straight across

Captain Thomas W. Custer, killed at the Battle of the Little Bighorn.

Captain George W. Wallace, killed in action at the Battle of
Wounded Knee.

our path, pursued by a wrathful figure wielding a flat lath.

"Why, Eliza!" cried the General to his ebony cook. "What on earth are you doing?"

"Doin'!" she echoed indignantly. "I'se gwine to beat dat onery critter plenty. He busted outta his pen, an' while I had my back turned makin' lemonade jest now, he come right into de kitchen an' grabbed a bunch of carrots right offen de table."

Meanwhile the object of her displeasure had paused under a tree and was munching away contentedly on the stolen goodies.

"That's Tom's pet calf," explained the General. "They're building it a big pen back of the stables, and he brought it over here for a few days."

Having finished its snack, the little buffalo ambled toward us, as tame as a dog, and permitted the General to lead it back to bed.

The rest of the evening was a real frolic. We danced, we sang, and we drank lemonade made with citric acid—that being the strongest beverage served in the General's home, as he himself was a teetotaler. He didn't object to his officers' imbibing strong liquor, provided they didn't do it while on duty, but woe betide any officer or enlisted man found intoxicated at that time. There has been much controversy and conjecture regarding the personal habits of this interesting man, but, while he loved the excitement of cards and dangers of all kinds, liquor of any sort was not in his line, at least while he was with his regiment.

What he did when he was on leave of absence no one knew nor cared.

The hop went on merrily, and we dropped hardtack crumbs all over the place, but no one fussed about it, least of all the Custers. As a matter of fact, they had little to be fastidious about, outside of the piano and a really beautiful collection of Indian relics given to the General by the chiefs of various tribes. These hung against the canvas-covered walls, but the carpenter's-horse tables, campstools, sketchy china assembled from many broken sets, bright rugs made from red flannel and discarded army uniforms, were more or less counted upon as army furnishings for everyone, irrespective of rank, because, with the regiment under canvas from six to nine months during the year and the constant changes of station, there was little incentive to make attractive homes. That came some years later.

The army mess was divided into two classes— the soldiers' and the officers'—the latter usually designed for the bachelors, but sometimes a married officer would invite an intimate friend to mess with him. Such was the case when Lieutenant Wallace took his meals with Mollie and Donald. It was an agreeable arrangement, and stimulated our feminine vanity to look well in the mornings.

Riding and Shooting

v

AT BREAKFAST next day, after the party at the Custers', I asked Donald, "What do the soldier's rations consist of?"

"Oh," he stated, wielding a jug of molasses, "pork bacon, canned or fresh salt beef or buffalo meat, bread, hardtack, peas, rice, hominy, and potatoes."

"What! No fresh beans, lettuce, or spinach?" I exclaimed.

"Listen to her," hooted Lieutenant Wallace. "Do you realize that it would cost the government a fortune to feed fresh vegetables to the army, with beans selling out here for fifty cents a quart, lettuce practically out of the market, and no spinach?"

"And how about desserts?"

"Oh," volunteered Donald, "they've plenty of bread puddings, dried-apple pies, and molasses cake, and in July they shake bullberries off the trees into their ponchos for tarts, and at Christmas we try to round up enough prairie chickens or venison for a feast."

"Yes," chimed in Mollie, "the officers don't get much more. True, we do have plovers, but they are so small they wouldn't go far in a regiment. As for fruit—last year, in an orgy of extravagance, I paid $1.50 for a dozen bananas in Bismarck."

"Not only that," amended Donald, "but last fall we paid twenty-five dollars for a barrel of apples that was shipped from Oregon by oxcart, and when they arrived, every one was frozen."

"Well," said I, "I wouldn't live in such a Godforsaken country, but as long as I am here, I want to see things." Turning to Lieutenant Wallace, I added, "Would you mind taking me to the stables this afternoon?"

"Glad to," he agreed, somewhat surprised, his blue eyes alert with sudden interest.

"Well, of all things," observed Mollie. "What do you want to go to such an unsavory place for?"

"Just for instance!" I flashed ambiguously, but the General had said to me the night before, in parting: "You must understand about horses. Get your brother-in-law or someone to take you to the stables once in a while and study them, if you really want to be a good rider."

So late that afternoon I tied on my little poke bonnet and, swishing my stiffly starched dimity dress, skipped and doubled my steps to keep abreast of the long strides of my escort as we crossed the parade ground.

Fort Lincoln, regimental headquarters, was only a six-troop post, so I asked inquisitively, "Why didn't they build this garrison large enough to house the whole regiment?"

"Because," explained Lieutenant Wallace, "all regiments have to be divided in order to take care of different sections of the country and to protect all settlers and railroad workers."

The barracks had been built on the side of the parade grounds nearest the river. Detached officers' quarters faced the opposite direction. Left of the parade grounds stretched a long granary and a small military prison called the "guard house." The prisoners, by the way, policed the garrison. Opposite these, and completing the square, were the quartermaster buildings, the commissary supplies, and adjutant office. Outside the garrison proper were frame stables built to house six hundred horses. Still farther back loomed the laundresses' homes. Some distance away Indian scouts and their families lived in log huts, but as we passed them I saw tepees erected beside the dwellings.

"The Indians sleep in those," explained Lieutenant Wallace, "as it makes them cough to sleep inside a house. They merely use the huts for storehouses."

Here also was the wide, level plain which served for special drills and parades. To the left of this was the one sutler's store permitted to every reservation, with a billiard room attached as a popular attraction.

We had reached the barracks when stable call sounded, and the soldiers swarmed out into the company streets like bees from a hive, where they formed into lines and marched away. I had always understood that armies traveled on their stomachs, but bugle calls seemed to be equally important, for they regulated the soldiers' every hour from reveille until taps.

So we went to the stables, and I launched a thousand questions ranging from those concerning horses' teeth to their shod feet.

"Thinking of buying a racing stable?" queried the young officer, his eyes twinkling.

"I might at that," I retorted pertly.

It was interesting to note the care given these creatures. The soldiers combed the horses' manes and tails to a feathery lightness and curried and fussed over their bodies as though they were human beings. When the task was completed these equine babies preened themselves with the vanity of a pretty woman and neighed lustily for their suppers.

They were led to their nursery stalls, fed, and put to bed, the fresh-smelling hay mattresses inviting sleep. The last rites of the ceremony consisted in the careful covering of these government pets with army blankets, because the nights were still chilly.

Well, the General certainly kept his promise to me, and he and Tom drove me like a galley slave during my riding and shooting lessons. Not only every day was I put through the paces, rain or shine, but several times during the twenty-four hours, according to their leisure minutes.

"Because," explained Tom, "once we leave for the campaign you won't have anyone to teach you."

After a few days I overcame my fear of horses and firearms and threw myself into the business of learning all about them with zeal and enthusiasm, partly through pride and partly through appreciation of the opportunity afforded me, because I could have found no better teachers than these two. My progress, on this account, was really quite rapid, and when one day Mrs. Custer said, "Autie and Tom are proud of your work and say that your shooting, especially, promises to be exceptional," I was hugely pleased and redoubled my efforts to learn. Soon they began to take me hunting, and one day, when I shot a bird from a branch, Tom forgot his manners and almost knocked me off my mount, slapping me on the back, and ejaculating, "Golly, what a shot!"

Meanwhile the campaign was boiling. Ten troops of the Seventh Cavalry and two companies of the Twentieth Infantry, with a small detachment of Indian scouts, under the command of General Custer were getting ready for the big push into the Black Hills of South Dakota, known today as the Sunshine State.

A camp, two miles south of Fort Lincoln, had been selected for the reunion of the regiment, where there was plenty of water, wood, grass, and a level country. Several weeks would be given over to intensive training of new recruits before the command could begin their march.

In the interim the garrison was seething with activity from the ordinary routine to extensive preparations in the quartermaster's department, the adjutant's office, the barracks, and even the hospital, and not a man was available until after parade. Across the stillness of the parade ground during the heat of the June day drifted the whistling and singing of the soldiers, punctuated from time to time with hearty guffaws, as the men weaved in and out of barracks, bent upon some errand. As I watched them hurrying here and there, I wondered how they stood the monotony of army life, with nothing to do after the close of a military day but sleep.

Each month, during the winter, a dance was given by a troop, which supplied its own soldier orchestra of accordions, harmonicas, jew's-harps, and sometimes banjos. To this came the four sturdy laundresses allotted to each troop, usually dragging small children and some carrying infants in arms, all of whom were deposited in the soldiers' cots while their mothers had their fling.

White maids from the officers' quarters were in great demand. Some of these were imported from the East or Midwest at trouble and expense to their employers, but, within from two to six weeks, according to their degree of pulchritude, they all married soldiers. This was discouraging, so the employment agencies were instructed to send only the homeliest females obtainable, and the army of knock-kneed, cross-eyed, crooked-teethed cooks and bottlewashers which hove into the garrison promised domestic security to the harassed housewives. However, their jubilance was short-lived, for, at the end of two months, every one of the freaks had landed a man. In fact, the homeliest of them all acquired a sergeant.

The negresses were fairly satisfactory as long as they would stay, but usually, with the exception of a few like Mrs. Custer's Eliza and Mollie's Iwilla, one devastating winter was enough to send them scampering back to the cotton fields.

The summer campaigns were welcomed gleefully by the soldiers. They broke the strain of the long, dreary cold and the cooped-up barrack intimacy of men from practically all over the world who would not always be in accord, and thus sometimes provoked feuds, especially among the French and Germans. Why foreigners sought military service so far from their homelands was never questioned, and they often finished their five-year term of enlistment without leaving a clue to their past. However, with the approach of summer, everyone relaxed and smiled again.

With the Franco-Prussians, the war was over, and the enemies shook hands. They even hunted and fished together. Adventure beckoned. There were streams to ford, valleys to be explored, and deep-shadowed, sweet-smelling ravines and perhaps big game invited, in the offing, or an exciting brush or two with the Indians. It was no wonder everyone was happy, and cracking jokes as gunny sacks of potatoes were tossed into the white-covered supply wagons along with other edibles, while trucks bristled with barrels of kitchen utensils, the axes and spades lashed to the sides. Hay and fodder were pitched into other wagons. Saddlers sewed up everything, including bedding, in canvas, which was then roped and tied inside the vans, followed by a hail of hay-filled pillows. Truckloads of guns and ammunitions were packed last, and surrounding the whole were hordes of joyous, barking dogs. Back of the corrals a herd of cattle waited to be taken on the march, to be killed when necessary, which was every other day. A note of keyed expectancy pervaded everything, and the horses pawed the ground destructively and sent forth paeans of neighing.

My shooting and riding instructions, perforce, had slackened a little, but someone was always trying me out, so on the nineteenth of June, the day preceding the march from Lincoln, when General Custer suggested that Mollie and I accompany him to camp and look over the ground, we accepted with alacrity. Mrs. Custer, it seemed, was busy with Eliza preparing lunch for the next day on a large scale, so we had to go without her.

We started off, bounded on all sides by ten or fifteen of the General's hunting dogs. As I looked at the man himself, I saw 170 pounds of bone and sinew swaying to every change of Dandy's gait, and wearing buckskin breeches, fringed on the sides, troop boots, a blue flannel shirt, loosened at the neck, and a red tie, topped by a small cap, his curls flying in the breeze. My imagination ran riot in these days, and, instantly, I visioned him as a reincarnation of one of Cortez' conquistadors.

He and Mollie lapsed into regimental conversation. They spoke mostly of the troops marching up from Rice the next day and kept referring to Captain Calhoun and his wife, the latter of whom

was the General's sister; also they harped upon
someone called "Gibby." This Gibby I had heard
of ever since my arrival, but only in a general way.
From what I gathered, he was an impudent young
devil who strained the leash of military discipline
to the breaking point with his pranks. He didn't
interest me, so I never bothered to ask about him.
However, when the General remarked, "Libbie
and I will be glad to see him. We've missed him
like the deuce," I was moved to inquire casually,
"Well, what about this Gibby? It seems to me
that his claim to fame lies mostly in his practical
jokes. What other attractions has he when his
jokes run out?"

Here my horse nosed a head or two forward,
leaving Mollie and the General for a moment in
the rear. When they caught up with me, the
General said, "We were speaking of Gibby. He is
something of a teaser, it's true, but a nice chap
and a splendid officer. But it's too bad."

"What's too bad?"

"Oh, he's such a shrimp—hardly tall enough to
meet the army requirements."

"Yes," continued Mollie, glancing up from under the visor of her forage cap (a riding fashion
affected by many cavalry women in those days),
"and that squint in his left eye."

"But it hasn't impaired his shooting any," defended the General, "and, of course, his harelip
doesn't help his appearance."

"No," conceded Mollie, "and being nearly bald,
too." She shook her head.

"Then for goodness' sake, what is there attractive about him?" I asked impatiently.

"Well, he has his good points," insisted the General.

"And he's heaps of fun," declared Mollie.

"But," I persisted, "he is so homely."

"Homely," echoed the General. Then teasingly he said, "Well, you wouldn't call Mr. Wallace a beauty, would you, and you like him pretty well?"

"No," I retorted, tossing my head, "but he isn't a—a shrimp, and—and he's awfully kind."

Here every dog in the pack stopped abruptly, with noses pointing, and all eyes were directed in front of us.

After a wintry spring, summer had burst upon the land with scorching heat. Sunning itself in the center of a deeply rutted wagon trail was the largest rattlesnake I had ever seen. Instantly we reined in our mounts. The General made signs for silence. With an odd sweep of his hand he seemed to lock the dogs in a state of complete inertia, for they neither budged nor barked. Then, like an eel, he slid from his horse and, throwing the reins to Mollie, turned toward the reptile. My hand flew to my mouth to keep from screaming, and my startled gaze darted to Mollie's face, which remained calm.

He approached the thing cautiously, treading as lightly as a cat. But the vibration warned it, for instantly it coiled, and its head raised venomously. The General began to circle it, walking faster and faster, gradually getting nearer and nearer the deadly fangs. Instinctively Mollie and I leaned forward in our saddles, our eyes glued upon those two living things, and it seemed as though we scarcely breathed. Then, suddenly, with a movement so swift that the eye could barely follow, the man bent, grasped the snake behind the neck, dashed it to the ground, and ground its head with the heel of his boot. After that he gave a single, sharp whistle, and the stonelike dogs came to life, barking, bounding, and sniffing at the striped thing in the grass. As he gathered up his reins again and mounted, the General turned to me and asked, teasingly, "What's the matter, Miss Katie? You're white as a sheet."

Several hours later, on our return, that snake was still wriggling.

The Coming of the Rice Detachment

vi

THAT NIGHT the entire garrison turned in early.
I slept little and awoke at reveille. Immediately
the post was seething with activity. Though the
march to camp was but trifling, the General wanted all tents pitched before the arrival of the Rice
detachment. While we gobbled our breakfast, the
striker was busy upstairs laying out Donald's
campaign outfit, which consisted of troop boots,
uniform trousers, a blue flannel shirt, a wide-
brimmed, black felt hat, cartridge belt, and
revolver.

The long roll call summoning the troops to turn
out had been sounded. Along Officers' Row horses
stood at hitching posts waiting impatiently to be
mounted. It was exciting to see their masters
come springing down the steps of their quarters,
fling themselves across those curried backs, and
animal and rider leap away. Ambulances were
provided for the officers' wives to follow the men
into camp.

Mollie and I piled into one and put Iwilla in the
boot along with a half-dozen hams she had cooked
the day before. Then we drove back of the barracks to join the troops just as assembly call broke
upon the air, and ranks were formed. Mrs. Custer,
in a black riding habit and a sensible wide-

Lieutenant Francis M. Gibson.

At camp on Big Creek. Dr. Dunbar, Mrs. Custer, Mr. Young, Brevet Lieutenant Colonel J. B. Weir, Mrs. Smith, General Custer, Mr. Lamborn (secretary U.P.R.R.), Mrs. McIntosh, Lieutenant Gibson.

brimmed hat shading her eyes, had taken her place beside the General at the head of the column.

"Boots and Saddles" (the call for mounting) was blared by the trumpet, and the regiment, as one man, sprang into their saddles. Behind the Custers rode the staff officers and orderlies, two by two, the troops marching in double file, followed by the Indian scouts and a few civilians. Then came the camp equipment and supply wagons, each drawn by two or four mules and driven by civilian teamsters who, by the way, ate alone. Back of these came the cattle, and finally a group brought up the rear with the quartermaster's detail. Hordes of dogs surrounded the column, the General and Tom owning forty of them. The cavalcade was so long that it took us nearly two hours to reach camp, but once there the wheels of military efficiency revolved like those of a well-oiled clock. Along the company streets tents were erected and furnished with cots, campstools, tin basins, buckets, dippers, and small mirrors swinging crazily from center poles; everything was done with a celerity that suggested the work of miracle hands.

The canvas of the commanding officer was set a little apart from the rest, but he enjoyed no more luxuries than his subalterns. The horses were picketed near the stream close by, but at night they were tied to long ropes that ran through the center of the company streets.

The large kitchen tent, rattling with tins, iron spits, pans, kettles, and cutlery, was already sending forth the aroma of cooking, and sniffing dogs hung about the flaps waiting to be flung scraps of food. Soldiers, carrying deep, narrow rubber buckets, made a continuous procession to the stream.

The horses were kicking up their heels and nibbling joyously at the young grasses, while the cattle, pastured a short distance away, busied themselves contentedly with the destruction of succulent green shrubs.

Midst the general excitement Iwilla emerged, staggering under a pile of hams. She paused in front of Lieutenant McIntosh's tent.

"Where's I gwine to put dese ham?" she panted.

"Why, give them to Sergeant Baumgarten," suggested Mollie.

"No, ma'am," she said violently, "I ain't a-goin' to give 'em to Sergeant Bumgarden, cause de las' time I done it, he switched on us, an' 'stead of my good hams we jess got de trash cooked by de sodgers." And with that she entered the tent and dumped her burden on Donald's cot.

What would have been the final settlement of this momentous question was left unanswered, for just then Lieutenant Weston (afterwards Quartermaster General) poked his head through the tent fly, crying, "They're here!" and we all rushed out.

Sure enough. We saw a column of soldiers rounding a bend in the road. They were in camping outfits and under the command of the ranking major. Sandwiched between the latter and a younger officer rode a woman, who turned out to be Margaret Calhoun, sister of the General and Tom. She was large and fine-looking, fair like her brothers, and sat her mount superbly.

At sight of the Rice detachment a roar of welcome went up from our men, and the band swung into "Garry Owen," the battle song of the Seventh Cavalry. Even before the column was brought to a halt soldiers and officers were surrounding the new arrivals, whose uniforms were white with dust. Finally, midst joyous confusion, the command halted, men slid from their mounts, Maggie Calhoun was hugged affectionately by her brothers and Mrs. Custer, and a vigorous, free-for-all mauling seemed to be in order. Such tossing of hats, such laughter, such questions! They grasped hands, grabbed each other's shoulders, and banged backs. I, as an outsider, watched fascinated, and again I was struck by that strong family tie that welded the army together. Not that they didn't have their disagreements—they certainly did, but they never amounted to much.

The same attitude seemed to prevail in the ranks, as was evident in the company streets where men, who had laughed and played, fought and sometimes cried together on previous campaigns, were playfully slugging each other in order to conceal their real emotions. Even the horses were nosing old friends, while the dogs lost no time in snarling at their old-time canine enemies.

The General was being constantly swallowed up by different groups, from which he emerged with the satisfied smile of a father welcoming home his children. In the background new tents rose as if by magic.

All this I noted as I stood alone beside Donald's tent. He and Mollie were completely absorbed and surrounded by their friends.

During my momentary isolation from regimental matters, my curiosity was aroused by some of the recent arrivals. One was a man with thick, almost white, hair, surmounting a young, clean-shaven face. He was compactly built, had a firm mouth and square chin, and walked with burro sure-footedness. Mollie had him buttonholed, and he was handing her a letter. Another of the lean, tall type wore a walrus mustache which gave him a rather melancholy air, until he smiled. Then his face lighted up with unsuspected animation. A third officer intrigued me greatly, possibly because I couldn't see his face. But his back was good to look upon, being broad and straight and boyish. He was some six feet in height, and around him was crowded a host of noisy youngsters. Some flung their arms across his wide shoulders, some jostled him affectionately, while others—like Lieutenants Weston, Varnum, and Donald — just gripped him in clumsy bear hugs. At that moment Mrs. Custer went hurrying by. The newcomer's long arm shot out, a slender hand caught hers and swung it for a second, then released it, but in that gesture I read a deep and understanding friendship.

Benny Hodgson must have been telling an amusing yarn, because everyone laughed, and the man with the attractive back emitted such a chuckle of contagious gaiety that I caught myself giggling.

"Want to meet him?" asked a voice at my elbow. I turned hastily.

"Oh, General," I gasped, "where did you come from?"

"Just over there, but you were so absorbed that you didn't see me," replied General Custer, his eyes twinkling. "Now you wait here." Before I could recover from my confusion he had joined that youthful group, slipped his arm through that of the man with the attractive back, and wheeled him in my direction. They were about the same height, these two, but the younger man was lighter in weight and brought with him a quality of life and movement that was electric. Straight as a Norway pine, this stranger unconsciously fell into step with his commanding officer. His campaign hat was worn at a rakish angle, and his clear, olive skin abutted in a mustache atop a mouth filled with flawless teeth. (I wonder why so many people in those old Western days had such splendid teeth. Perhaps the hardtack, tough venison, and sinewy buffalo meat had something to do with it.) The long legs of the boy lieutenant swung from his hips with the same jerky stiffness of all saddle-bound men of the plains. Impish daring danced in his large brown eyes, but it was his smile that held you with a warmth that reached out to every man, woman, child, and animal alike.

The two men halted beside me.

"Miss Garrett," began the General with mock gravity, "may I present the ugly duckling of the regiment—Mr. Frank Gibson—called Gibby."

Gibby—I caught my breath, and bewilderment poured through me. He and Mollie said he was a —a shrimp—a—a—— Then the truth rushed over me, and I flung the General a withering glance. So they had played football with my credulity. Well, I'd show them.

By this time the subject of my thoughts had doffed his hat, disclosing a wealth of wavy, dark hair, and, with the battery of his engaging smile turned upon me, murmured in deep, pleasant tones, "We've waited for you a long time, Miss Garrett, and I hope you're going to like us."

"Oh, I'm sure to," I rejoined, smiling.

"Do you—er——"

"Yes, I do."

"Do what?"

"Shoot and ride." Then recalling a habit of the enlisted men, I added banteringly, "I can't chew yet, but give me time."

The dancing light in his eyes became a veritable rumba, as he challenged, "So you do, and—er— you don't. Well, when will you prove your prowess in the field?"

"Any time you say," airily.

Then we laughed, which broke one spell and started another. He was big and strong and magnificent, and I was small and young and blue-eyed. No wonder the magic of the moment held us and that a flash of miraculous sympathy and understanding was born between us with the meeting of our eyes. It was all too wonderful, and finally when we sighed and returned to earth the General had tiptoed away.

It sounds as though my family had completely abandoned me, but in reality these happenings occurred within a few minutes, and now as Mollie wended her interrupted way toward me—for she was pumphandled every few feet by some old friend of the Rice contingent—I could have slain her for injecting herself into the most romantic moment of my life. However, I gave vexation pause as she said, "Come on—lunch'll be served presently, and I've seated Donald under that tree over there. He'll be all right soon."

"What's the matter with him?" Gibby and I asked in unison.

"Oh, he got kicked by a fractious horse. Come on."

Mess call sounded just then, and the combined neighing of horses, barking of dogs, and braying of mules became deafening. It was music to the ears of human beings as well, because everyone had breakfasted sketchily. Hence our appetites were knife-blade sharp. Now that I was adapting myself to this rugged, simple life, I began to like it and everything about it. For instance, I could swallow a certain amount of buffalo meat and was training my stomach to tolerate the gamy flavor of venison.

Great activity was emanating from the kitchen tent, while the ringing sound of tin cups and plates sent people scattering in anticipatory groups, seated everywhere.

We finally reached the tree—or rather the huge bush—in the shade of which Donald was reclining, his injured leg stretched out stiffly.

"Broken?" queried Lieutenant Gibson.

"No, just shinbone bruised," replied Donald, but he winced when he moved.

By this time the carpenter's-horse tables were being quickly joined together, and on the bare planks the tin dishes rattled invitingly, while Eliza and Iwilla, with several other helpers, refilled the ever-emptying board.

The Custers and Calhouns were seated together on the ground, the General in a posture of complete relaxation. He had a habit of throwing himself prone on the grass for a few minutes' rest and resembled a human island, entirely surrounded by crowding, panting dogs. Captain and Mrs. Yates were near by, for Annie and Mrs. Custer were old and very dear friends. The Moylans and McDougalls had their coteries, the Algernon Smiths theirs, and other groups were scattered among the tables.

To ours came Brevet Colonel Benteen, the man with the mane of white hair and eyes of great brilliance, and a precision of glance that was quietly piercing. He was Lieutenant Gibson's troop commander, and between these two one sensed deep mutual respect and confidence. Lieutenant Godfrey, later General Godfrey, he of the walrus mustache, also joined us and kept calling Lieutenant Gibson, "George," though that was not

Brevet Colonel Frederick W. Benteen.

Lieutenant Edwin S. Godfrey, later a General.

his name. I liked Lieutenant de Rudio, too. He was charming and jolly, and we had really the merriest kind of a picnic, despite Donald's evident pain.

Suddenly the General rose and motioned for silence.

Said he, "The doctor has a surprise for you. You see, he did a favor for a ranchman on the march, and he made him a very welcome gift."

"Oh, what was the favor?" called inquisitive Mollie.

"And the surprise?" chorused other feminine voices.

"As to the favor," volunteered Dr. Lord, "I merely relieved him of a gangrenous leg. And the surprise—well, wait till you see."

Here Eliza and "Rise" and their retinue were passing plates around, upon which appeared sandwiches and onions—of all things—onions, two to each person. My face fell with disgust, yet, on second thought, I realized that I hadn't seen one since I reached the plains. Could this be the surprise? Evidently it was, judging from the howls of joy that arose at the sight of them.

"Onions," ejaculated Captain Ilsley. "What a treat."

"Onions," shouted Benny Hodgson. "Nectar for the gods."

"Yes," said the doctor. "He gave me two big sacks of them."

"Gosh-a-mighty," exclaimed Captain French, "we haven't even seen an onion in six months," and one and all fell upon that raw, common vegetable, devouring it as though it had been the rarest of fruits.

After lunch the trumpet sounded, and all the officers gathered in and around General Custer's tent, where a council was held. Donald, however, was in such pain that the doctor insisted upon examining his leg, with the result that the sufferer was ordered back to the Lincoln hospital for a few days, where the injured member could be treated. Of course, this meant that Mollie, Iwilla, and I would have to return also. Youth is labeled selfish, and, though really distressed about Donald, I hated to leave camp, which, within a couple of hours, had become a paradise for me, proving what havoc a pair of velvet brown eyes and stalwart shoulders could wreak upon a girl. But my reprieve was at hand, for Mrs. Custer came hurriedly forward.

"Don't take Katie," she pleaded with Mollie. "Let her stay with me until you and Mr. McIntosh return."

"Oh, thank you, Mrs. Custer, but I think I'd better go with them," I murmured deceitfully, hoping my opinion would be overruled. And it was.

Mrs. Custer threw me a searching look, then continued with teasing insistence.

"Nonsense." She gave my arm a knowing little squeeze. "You could do nothing—and we need you much more here."

Mollie readily agreed, and, rather guiltily, I watched the ambulance jog away with them, Donald protesting that there was nothing the matter with him. "Rise" again occupied the boot, clutching two leftover hams.

Immediately a tent was pitched next to the Custers', but, when I realized that I was to sleep in this flimsy canvas out on the open plain, I grew uneasy, despite the assurance that nothing could harm me with a sentinel patrolling in front of it all night.

Finally Tom Custer suggested with a perfectly straight face, "Suppose we put a padlock on the inside for you."

"Good idea," seconded the General, without winking an eyelash. "Will that suit you?"

"Yes," I replied, completely satisfied. "Then I'll be safe."

So a soldier was solemnly ordered to undertake the ridiculous job. Several officers gathered about to see the fun, and not one cracked a smile. It took years to live down that incident.

The night was gorgeous, and the full moon made silvery paths through the company streets, which were barricaded at both ends against any sudden attacks from wild animals or hostiles. The band played for a while, little groups gathered, all the dogs were safely tied up for the night, and officers and enlisted men relaxed.

Lieutenant Gibson and I noted these things but vaguely. We were seated apart from the others and completely absorbed in the marvelous discovery of each other, while the sweet aroma from a blooming wild-rose bush near by stole into our nostrils and combined with the magic of the moon-glow to hypnotize us into the delusion that life was just one prolonged ecstasy.

Tattoo had sounded, followed by taps, which the echoing bluffs flung back at us, as clear as a bell. From the distant hills came the protesting howls of coyotes, for, curiously enough, the notes of brass instruments seemed to produce in these small, wild wolves something akin to pain.

But Frank and I were oblivious to everything but ourselves and had lapsed already into the usual sentimental platitudes such as, "I wish this night would last forever," my cue being, "Oh, do you feel that way too?" so that the sentinels called out the hours to deaf ears as far as we were concerned, and it was not until a slender figure stood before us that we awoke and saw Mrs. Custer smiling down upon us. In confusion, Frank sprang to his feet, and I fussed consciously with a ruffle at my neck.

"Come, children," urged my hostess, "it's late, and a bite of supper is waiting for you before you turn in."

So the three of us trailed over to the Custers' tent, which loomed like a specter in the white light, and there we found cold plover, hardtack, cold coffee, and some of Eliza's wild-plum jam, as bitter as gall, but spicy with meats.

It is strange how long it takes sometimes to say good night, and Frank and I had no idea of the hour as we stood outside my tent whispering until the General's voice, coming from his own canvas, called out, "Hey, you two! Tomorrow's another day, you know."

So my young officer scurried off to the bachelors' quarters, and I, snuggling under my army blankets a few minutes later, relived the events of the wonderful day, which deferred my sleep, but when once I closed my eyes I didn't open them even in the bright light of early dawn, until an orderly scratched at my tent fly, saying, "Mrs. Custer's compliments, Miss Garrett, and breakfast will be ready in fifteen minutes."

Half awake, I crawled out of my cot, but the ting of fresh water against my face opened my eyes with alacrity. I dragged on my clothes, dampish from the dew, combed my hair hastily before the tiny mirror, and presented myself promptly at the Custers' tent.

AFTER BREAKFAST the men all disappeared, and we saw no more of them until luncheon. But we had plenty to do. The women gathered about the Custer tent with their sewing, and we indulged in an orgy of military gossip. Some of the regiment had already served in the restless south, and it was rumored that, following the campaign, these troops would be replaced by a detachment from Dakota, which in turn would be sent to quell riots, break up illicit distilleries, look into the activities of the Ku Klux Klan, and really act in the capacity of constabulary police.

Maggie Calhoun was a lot of fun and had the qualities of her brothers which made friends readily, and I am sure that Mrs. Custer could not have loved any member of her own family more than she did "Sister Margaret," as she called her.

Mrs. Custer herself plied a skillful needle, and made all of the General's shirts, and as she sat basting and cutting in front of the tent she laughingly told us of an incident that happened at Yankton.

The General was away somewhere, and she was in the midst of making him some nightshirts, so, as Lieutenant Gibson was nearly the former's build, she drafted him into service for the fittings.

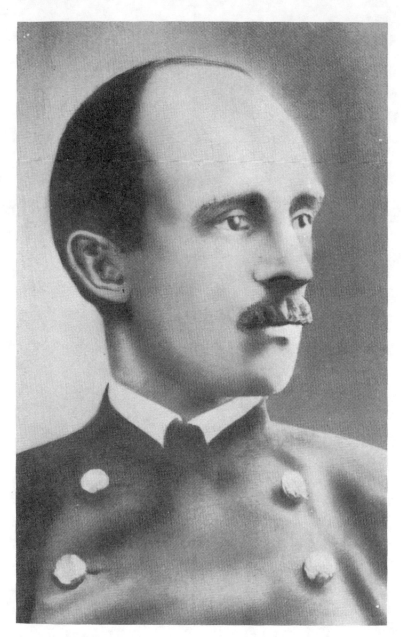

Lieutenant Charles A. Varnum, later a Colonel.

"Well," she began, waving her scissors, as I reached for a pair of the General's socks that needed darning, "Mr. Varnum happened to come in as my model stood at solemn attention with a nightshirt over his uniform. He started to laugh and bet Gibby five dollars that he wouldn't dare show himself in the street like that, whereupon the youngster pulled away from me, scattering all my pins, darted down the steps, and was out into the street like a shot, where he paraded in front of the hotel. People pointed, stared, and laughed, but it didn't faze him a bit, and finally he came back and collected the bet."

Then turning to me, she instructed, "Don't mend that sock with a drawing string, but darn it, my dear."

I looked down woefully at the lump in my hand, but Charlotte Moylan came to my rescue.

"Here, let me show you," she offered. She sewed beautifully and subsequently taught me many useful things. In fact, every one of these practical women added greatly to my store of general and specialized knowledge, and how we enjoyed these impromptu sewing bees! Mrs. Custer welcomed them even more than the rest of us, because for five years she was the only woman in the regiment who followed the troops into camp during campaign preparations, so at times she had been very lonely.

To me this was a thrilling adventure, and I would sit at the feet of these new friends and drink in thirstily their tales of the unfolding West.

"Tell me," I begged, "when did the Seventh Cavalry come into existence?"

"Oh, in 1866," replied Mrs. Custer. "It was organized at Fort Riley, Kansas, and designated by the War Department, the Seventh Cavalry. It was commanded by three West Pointers—Colonel Andrew Jackson Smith, Lieutenant Colonel George Armstrong Custer——"

"Colonel?" I broke in, surprised.

"Yes," Mrs. Yates hastened to explain, "but he was a Major General during the Civil War. However, when the war was over, and this new regiment was formed, he became its Lieutenant Colonel, but retains his title of General—that is termed Brevet."

"Oh, I see," I murmured, the matter as clear as mud.

"And," continued Mrs. Custer modestly, yet with pardonable pride, "Autie was only twenty-four when he became a General, and he and General Smith and General Gibbs, the third officer in command of the Seventh Cavalry, fought through the entire war."

"Marvelous," I exclaimed, "and then what happened to the regiment?"

"Oh," replied Mrs. Custer, laughing, "we prowled all up and down Oklahoma, Kansas, Nebraska, and Dakota, chasing Indians."

I gasped, "Oh, but they're still doing it, and aren't you afraid for your men?"

"Of course we are," came the unanimous reply.

I looked into those clear, quiet eyes—blue,

brown, grey—with amazement, then realized that every woman is an actress when it comes to concealing her feelings.

But now Mrs. Custer was launched upon the past activities of the regiment, and little by little I absorbed the story of the Battle of the Washita, where "Garry Owen," the battle song of the Seventh, was born. This engagement, described by Captain Gibson (then a lieutenant) in the *History of the Seventh Cavalry*, was fought in the dead of winter.

Mrs. Custer dwelt upon the hatred of the young hostiles for the white men and the perfidy of their wily chiefs, who, though feigning great friendship for the army and settlers, secretly encouraged the fiery bucks to perpetrate such outrages as murder, arson, and rapine.

Again and again the government protested against these maraudings, and again and again the oily chiefs promised prompt punishment for the malefactors and a cessation of these atrocities, yet these things continued even more flagrantly until the Indians, growing bolder, began to carry off young white women. Then General Sheridan decided to act and summoned General Custer to take command. But the situation was fraught with triggerlike difficulties, for it was late autumn, and arctic winter could be expected to swoop down upon the land at any moment. In spite of the climatic menace, however, a campaign at this time had its advantages. During the summer months the Indians, ponies, bags and baggage, could evaporate overnight, but in the winter they hibernated in their wickiups, and so were easier to locate.

General Custer joined his command at Bluff Creek, the entire regiment, with the exception of L troop, being present at the time and eager for activity. The settlers and traders welcomed the idea of a winter campaign, for they charged $9.00 apiece for flannel shirts, $1.00 a pair for plain cotton socks, and everything else in proportion, and, in the excitement, no one caviled at prices.

So, at four o'clock one morning in November, 1868, the command left Camp Supply and with eight hundred men marched to Beaver Creek in the snow while, strangely enough, the snowbirds were singing blithely. From then on intense hardships, physical suffering, and bitter privations were endured.

The detachment, with fur collars turned up, finally reached the Washita River, where they rode into the fury of the storm, the snow coming down in such heavy clouds that even the keen eyes of the Osage Indian guide could not penetrate it. Here General Custer himself rode at the head of the column and guided it, by compass, to Wolf Creek, where they camped.

Next day they resumed their march and, after four days, arrived at the Canadian River. Here, Major Joel Elliott, with three troops, was sent out to look for trails, while the rest of the command prepared to ford the river, which was extremely treacherous not only from ice floes, but quicksands.

The Major had left before dawn, and all day

long the command waited for news of him. Finally Corbin, a scout, reached camp on an exhausted mount, with the news that the Indian trail, only one day old, had been found. Tired as he was, the man only waited for a bite of hard bread and coffee, and a fresh horse to return to Elliott with the assurance that the troops would join him as soon as possible. From that time on the command was stripped of every hindrance to rapid transit. They cut loose from the wagon train and took just as little in the way of rations, forage, and blankets as possible. Plenty of ammunition, of course, was necessary, as they knew that a battle was imminent within a few hours.

The train, which was to follow them as rapidly as it could, was in charge of Lieutenant Mathey, with a detail of men to afford it proper protection, and in less than half an hour after Corbin left the troops were on the march.

At this point in her story, Mrs. Custer dropped her sewing in her lap.

"Think of it," she said with combined pride and wistfulness, "there they were with little food, a single blanket each, and only the sky for covering in the midst of a severe winter—many suffering from frostbitten hands and feet. All day long they ploughed through the snow, with not a rein drawn, not a moment of rest taken, not a morsel of food having passed their lips since morning, and not one word of complaint from the whole command." At nine o'clock that night they caught up with Major Elliott, and one hour of rest and refreshment was taken. Then the march resumed.

They traveled all through the night and reached the Indian village at dawn. The Cheyennes, winter-locked in their wickiups, were taken by complete surprise, and, with the band playing "Garry Owen," the white men attacked the sleeping settlement.

Captain Hamilton, in command of a squadron, had, according to turn, been detailed to defend the supply and munition wagons, but he went to Custer.

"I want to ask a favor, sir," began the young officer diffidently.

"Well, well—what is it?" demanded the General impatiently.

"I—I wonder if you would permit me to lead my own squadron—in battle."

"Certainly not," snapped Custer, jerking at him one of his flashing glances. "Your detail for today is the wagon train. Why should another officer be deprived of his right to fight, in order to please you?"

"Because," persisted Captain Hamilton, "though every officer of this command is most efficient, they do not know my men. I have trained them. They're used to me. They know every intonation of my voice, every gesture of my hand, and I feel— I know—that they will fight better under me than under anyone else."

The General stooped swiftly, grabbed a bunch of snow, and began rubbing it against his frost-bitten cheek, then he stroked his chin thoughtfully, as his eyes roamed over that great expanse of dead, white stillness, for all warning bugle calls had been suppressed.

Then he spoke slowly, "Captain Hamilton, I appreciate your feelings, but I cannot grant your request—in fairness to the others—unless you can persuade another officer to take over the train detail for you."

"Thank you, sir," gasped the captain, his handsome face beaming. He dashed off to find Lieutenant Mathey. "Hey, Bible Thumper," he accosted the young Frenchman, "do me a favor, will you? Take over the wagon-train detail for me today."

Mathey opened his big brown eyes. "I will not. I'm looking for glory and excitement, too," and he rubbed his hand over his eyes.

The captain was quick to note the gesture.

"Look, Gus," he pursued seriously, "you're so snow-blinded now that you have to trust entirely to your horse. What good will you be in the ranks? Besides, unless I miss my guess, you'll have plenty of fighting defending the wagon train."

The lieutenant pressed his fingers to his eyes again, hesitated, then reluctantly admitted, "Yes, I've a bad case of snow blindness, but I've been hoping that it would clear. Doesn't seem to, though."

"Then you will take over the train detail?" eagerly.

"Guess I'll have to."

So this left Captain Hamilton free to command his own squadron.

Mrs. Custer paused, and all eyes were fixed on her.

"Well," I broke in anxiously, "well?"

She sighed, then resumed, "Well, he did so—with great brilliance and glory—then suddenly his horse wheeled and dashed away from the detachment, the rider sitting upright, his face ashen, his eyes staring. And when the animal came to an ·abrupt stop Captain Hamilton slid from his saddle into the snow—dead. Dr. Lord hurried to him and found that he had been killed instantly by a bullet through the heart, yet so accustomed was he to the gait of his mount that he had ridden a number of yards after death."

"Oh," I gasped, "how awful—perfectly awful," and unexpectedly I found myself sniveling over the passing of a total stranger. No one spoke, nor offered me a handkerchief, so I just reached for a pair of the General's socks and dried my eyes. Still my curiosity was not appeased.

"And—and were there any other casualties?" I asked.

"Major Elliott became separated from the command while chasing some escaping Indians, and he, too, was killed. Colonel Barnitz was supposed to have received his death wound, but survived. Tom Custer and Lieutenant March were wounded slightly, and Colonel Benteen had his horse shot from under him by a son of Chief Black Kettle, whom he afterwards killed. There were in all, I believe, killed and wounded, in enlisted men and officers, about thirty-five, but the soldiers wiped

Major Joel H. Elliott, killed at the Battle of the Washita.

Captain Louis M. Hamilton, killed at the Battle of the Washita.

out the Cheyennes, who lost heart after Black Kettle's death. It was a terrific battle, for the Indians, though taken unawares, fought with valor, and there were many hand-to-hand encounters.

"The troops captured nearly a thousand horses, ponies, and mules in good condition, some two or three hundred saddles of fine workmanship, thousands of arrows, about six hundred buffalo robes, close to five hundred blankets, seven hundred pounds of tobacco, all their supply of buffalo meat, meal, flour, rifles, revolvers, hundreds of pounds of bullets, over a thousand pounds of lead, nearly six hundred pounds of powder, hatchets, tomahawks, and bows, and, best of all, they rescued two white children who had been held prisoners."

Of course, this was an old story to the other women, but to me it was not only new and appalling, but it confused my sense of justice. Doubtless the white men were right, but were the Indians entirely wrong? After all, these broad prairies had belonged to them.

"It was all terrible," I managed to say, "but how wonderful to get back the children."

All nodded solemnly.

Just then mess call put an end to the morning needle club, and hungry men and horses came galloping into camp from every point of the compass.

Days in Camp

viii

AFTER LUNCH, eaten on the grass or under bushes,
Lieutenant Gibson and I rode into Lincoln. Donald was much better, but, to be on the safe side,
the doctor kept him in the hospital for a day or
two longer, which fretted the patient almost to
tears.

I stayed on with the Custers, and the happy
hours sped by all too quickly. Riding and shooting
in the clear, singing breeze with the air full of
bird notes stirred one's blood with the joy of living.
Mrs. Custer, Maggie Calhoun, and I would canter
over to the rifle range and watch the shooting
with appreciative eyes. What the men could do
with those old carbines, which went bad after the
second firing, was nothing short of a miracle.

Tom Custer made me shoot at an improvised
target away from the big range, and, nothing
loath to show off before Lieutenant Gibson, I did
my very best.

Tom was awfully proud of my skill, and Lieutenant Gibson was duly impressed, which satisfied my vanity.

Those few days together ripened the friendship
between Mrs. Custer and myself amazingly, and
when I look back I realize what a wonderful woman she was. Highly intellectual, she never forced

it upon anyone, yet often, when she had a few moments alone, one would find her scanning a French or German grammar, or perhaps one of the classics. Never did I know her to criticize anyone unkindly, and she seemed to make both the troubles and happiness of her husband's officers her personal interest. While there were some splendid and ranking officers in the regiment with excellent records, yet General Custer's outstanding personality and dash made such an imprint upon his fellow officers that this organization was known, and always will be, as Custer's Seventh.

Followed another night of witchery, and the encircling land pressed near and around us, while the all-pervading moonshine, steeped in platinum and shadows, fell benignly athwart the camp.

Mrs. Custer and Maggie clamored for some music, and here, of course, was where Mollie always shone, but, during her absence, it seemed to devolve upon me to replace her, so I played on my guitar and sang as Lieutenant Gibson stretched himself lengthily on the grass beside me. Several others brought out their banjos, and under the canopy of sky, frescoed by the Milky Way, we achieved a simple contentment that no one outside of that little isolated group could understand— not even I, six weeks ago. But slowly my Eastern life was receding into the background, and its comforts, crowded streets, and congested spaces were becoming less alluring to me.

Mrs. Custer was seated on a campstool, and the General lounged on the ground beside her—minus his dogs, because, by his orders, every canine had been tied up against night brawling with wolves and coyotes. But finally the fun and music ceased, and the sandman began to make his tardy rounds. Weary officers yawned surreptitiously, said good night, parted the flies of their tents, and vanished within.

I didn't trouble to light a candle but slid into my nightgown and rolled into bed, where I lay for a long time in happy, wakeful dreaming, the echoing voices of the sentinels lulling me into a state of contented security. The moon had sunk itself in a cloud, and I had just begun to drowse, when something roused me again to complete wakefulness. Just what it was I didn't know, because there was no noise, and yet some sixth sense held me taut. I sat up in bed and peered strainingly into the darkness, then my heart skipped a beat, for surely, over there in in a corner of my tent, something was moving. I did not scream, because it was no small matter to arouse a whole camp in the dead of night, but I held my breath and listened. Then, for a flashing moment, the moon stabbed through, and I heaved a sigh of relief.

One of the dogs had got loose and was prowling about the camp. These canine nocturnal visitors seemed to have a yen for my society, and my mind reverted to the mastiff episode at the ranch house. However, this wasn't quite the same thing, for the poor soldier responsible for the liberty of this army dog would be severely punished on account of negligence. I felt sorry for the unlucky man, and, still steeped in romance and sentiment from the day before, I permitted some of it to spill over onto the stranger. Perhaps he, too, was young, I mused, with a mother and sweetheart far away, for whom he yearned. I sighed at the thought, and then an idea trickled into my brain. If I managed to keep the dog in my tent until morning, he could then wriggle out and join the pack without being missed. So I raised myself on my elbow and very softly began to call the dog by every name I knew, from Tom's pet "Brandy" to "Tige," but he didn't respond to any of these. Still I didn't relinquish my efforts.

Finally, cautiously he approached me, and I reached under my pillow for the piece of hardtack I kept tucked away in case I should wake up in the night, hungry. As he came toward the cot I held out the tidbit, thinking that if he ate it he might slump down contentedly and go to sleep.

After sniffing it, however, he snatched it and, wandering toward the tent fly, slid to his belly, and nosed out of the canvas. Just then a rifleshot rang out, the echoing hills splitting the stillness like thunder.

Instantly the camp was awake. What had happened? Had a buffalo herd invaded the place? Had Indians attacked us? Breathless with suspense, I whipped into my dressing gown and stepped into the company street. The whole detachment was turning out in sundry stages of dishabille—some buckling on carbine belts, some carrying firearms, some wide-eyed with alarm, others blinking groggily from under half-open lids. Lieutenant Gibson cleared the intervening space in a bound and stood beside me, a revolver in his hand. Mrs. Custer was peering out of her tent, while the General in a large plaid dressing gown was demanding sternly of the patrolling sentinel the cause of the commotion.

The man saluted and stepped aside, revealing an object sprawled in the street. He said, "I just shot a wolf, sir, coming out of the young lady's tent." What happened after that? Why, the General and I changed sleeping quarters, and I bunked in with Mrs. Custer for the remainder of the night.

The next day Donald and Mollie returned, and my tent was pitched next to theirs.

The precious moments were racing by, and soon the troops would be on the march, so, when the thoughtful Custers decided to give a *fête champêtre*, the news was received with enthusiasm, though it was really planned more for the women detained at Lincoln by children, and who could only get out to camp occasionally in the daytime, than for us, already there.

And what preparations ensued! Soldiers who had distinguished themselves in rifle practice or military tactics were given the day off to scour the plains for plover or prairie chickens, which liberty they welcomed as a schoolboy does a holiday. The few women of the camp vied with each other in spying out patches of wild strawberries. Of course, it took a million of them to make a showing, so we increased the quantity by making them into jam.

The morning of the affair was perfect, the air so clear it seemed to shine, and the prairies a riot of color from the devil's-paintbrush and masses of flowering weeds.

Mollie and Mrs. Custer and I ranged these spaces, ducking bees that zoomed in and out of the bushes, and gathered armfuls of dew-dipped, spicy-smelling roses. These we placed decoratively in deep, rubber buckets, serving as vases, which we pilfered not only from the officers' tents but from the kitchen outfit as well. The two companies of the Twentieth Infantry entered into the spirit of the entertainment with glee, and, incidentally, they proved to be a valuable addition to the expedition not only from a military standpoint, but were most congenial as well.

Came the late afternoon, and with it, ambulances, buckboards, and rigs of all descriptions, teeming with the garrison crowd, who brought rations galore.

The influx of wives and overnight guests caused a temporary shortage of canvas shelter, so the bachelors were routed out of their so-called quarters and herded together in sketchy tent accommodations, from which would emerge loud protests of, "Where's my razor?" and "I'm shy a boot." These articles seemed to have been mislaid or dropped in hasty transmission. However, they were eventually recovered from sundry wheel ruts, cactus plants, or just the plain prairie, and the evicted ones regained their good humor and had a grand time.

As for clothes? I was fairly well equipped, just coming from the East, but the other women dug down in their army chests and resurrected what finery they could, but no one would have taken a fashion prize.

However, with a full moon and the broad prairies for a ballroom, a regimental band, and feet itching to dance, what more could we want? At the other end of camp a long table was set up, and a rubber bucket containing wild flowers marked the joining of each set of carpenter's horses. Handkerchiefs served to cover the bare planks in lieu of doilies, which gave something of a festive touch, the men gallantly declaring the effect to be ravishing.

Mrs. Custer received us in a faded muslin frock of ancient vintage, which she called her "valentine dress," "because," she explained, "I've had it since the year one."

I was the belle of the ball, not because of my irresistible charm, but because I was the only unmarried woman present. The beautiful daughters of General Sturgis were both away, as were the two attractive Merrill girls, and Zoe Godfrey, the pretty sister of Lieutenant Godfrey, was back at Rice fighting the Missouri mosquitoes along with her sister-in-law, all of which boosted my popularity, though Annie Yates with her lovely dark eyes and featherweight feet ran me a close second. Handsome, blond Captain Yates was justly proud of her. Anyway, the hop was on, and did we dance? Ah, me—what space for the square dances and the Virginia reel and, best of all, the waltz with the man one loved!

Romance was abroad that night, and it seemed to me that I could have floated away forever on the strains of the "Beautiful, Blue Danube," so exquisitely rendered by the band.

Under the clear, quiet sky, beyond the outskirts of civilization, for practically no ranches existed west of Bismarck before 1876, it was hard to realize how really isolated we were, yet Fort Lincoln and Bismarck comprised the white man's only oases in a desert wilderness stretching for miles in every direction and surrounded, though at a distance, by hostiles of various tribes. There were other small posts scattered here and there, but their military force and equipment were pitifully inadequate.

However, seated on a bank of the little stream and fluttering a tiny, senseless fan, with Lieutenant Gibson beside me, I was oblivious to everything but my own happiness. A spell, woven in the starlight, seemed to reach down towards the sweet-smelling earth and toss into my lap the things that my soul craved. My slender shoulder nestled against a broad one, and my small hand was suddenly in a strong, young grip, and I couldn't remember how it got there, but laughing brown eyes held mine prisoners, and nothing else mattered.

It might have been lunar madness that en-

meshed my man and me, but, when we finally
joined the others, I had signed up for a permanent
enlistment with the Seventh Cavalry. I, who only
a few weeks ago vowed never to tie my life to any
impoverished lieutenant as Mollie had done, never
to forsake the culture and green vegetables of the
East for the crudities, hardtack, and perpetual
canned beans of the army and the West. Yet here
I was surrendering myself with unmaidenly eager-
ness, in a shockingly short period (as my sister
Sally would have accused me), into the very jaws
of a rough, tough existence. Had I no pride? No
—in this instance, none whatever.

When Lieutenant Gibson and I reappeared, everyone was at table, and the feasting and merry-
making were well under way. We were both of
us more or less distrait, and from time to time I
could feel Mrs. Custer's eyes upon us and caught
an occasional glance from Donald, half knowing,
half speculative, but Mollie, entertaining a couple
of men at once, was in her element and paid us
little attention.

Later when the remains of the spread had been
cleared away and the band had turned in, everyone clamored for just a few songs to wind up the
evening, so Mollie and I sang to the accompaniment
of our guitars, joined by a chorus of bass and tenor
voices, finally finishing with "Tenting Tonight."

From boisterous hilarity, those who couldn't
sing lapsed into silence and listened. Many times
in after years my mind drifted back to that night
because, with the exception of two troops stationed

at Fort Totten, the entire regiment was together for the last time before the tragedy of '76. Blanched moonlight flooded the plains. Figures of men and women were silhouetted against the white tents. Soft breezes rustled the prairie grasses, blew across the bronzed faces of the men, and lifted the ruffles of the women's frocks. Peace proclaimed itself from the hills and dales and level plains, yet as I glanced up into that crooked, lunar face, resembling an ivory soup plate, it seemed to look down upon our little coterie with a cold, sardonic leer. It was an imagined expression, of course, which my own happiness quickly dispelled.

Mollie and Donald received our breath-taking news with genuine satisfaction. The men gripped hands tensely, and Mollie, blinking away the moisture in her eyes, planted a vagrant kiss somewhere in the region of my ear, as she commented boastfully, "I'm not surprised, because I planned all this before you came out."

That was Mollie. No matter what happened in the family, she always claimed to have had a hand in it, provided the event was a pleasant one. But I let it pass without comment. "However," she added discouragingly, "you'll get Hell from the family." I could see her already preening herself for battle. At least she would be on my side if the worst came to the worst, I consoled myself.

Finally, alone in my tent, and wakefulness sparring with sleep, I blew out my candle and sat huddled on my cot, my arms locking my knees.

One moment tremulous joy, sweet as spring

water, bubbled through my being, then I permitted a cowardly quivering to rise to the surface of that water and turn it brackish because, unlike Mollie, I didn't revel in family feuds. Of course, I realized that this new slant to my life was altogether alien to my former one, yet Frank Gibson was worth it—well worth it. Mollie, in general, had a very level head, but where romance was concerned she was so radical that I wished I had someone else to confide in.

Here, as though in answer to my thought, a light step crackled the dry grass in front of my tent, and a soft voice, lowered almost to a whisper, asked, "Are you awake, Katie?"

Mrs. Custer—and like a flash I was out of bed and across the tent to the fly. Like schoolgirls indulging in a forbidden midnight feat we sat huddled together on the cot in the lightless tent and whispered.

"You know?" I asked.

"Of course, I know. I knew tonight even before Gibby told me. You don't mind, do you? Outside of your brother and sister, he wanted Autie and me to hear it first."

"No," I replied, "I'm glad." I added, hesitatingly, "Mollie is dear, and all that, but I need— need——"

"Calmness, now, and sober thought," finished Mrs. Custer, which showed how well she knew my brilliant, fascinating sister, and she laughed softly under her breath.

What a sane and satisfactory talk we had! She

did not paint army life in the gay colors of an artist's brush. On the contrary, she spoke seriously and bared every phase of it, from the necessity sometimes of associating with uncongenial people, down to living in drab stockade posts. She stressed the insufficient pay of an officer, compelling many sacrifices; she pointed out the months of loneliness for the women during the prolonged campaigns, the lack of comforts, even the prospect of going hungry at times; she spoke of dangers, real and imaginary—yet nothing mattered if you loved your man. Her face was expressive of deep reflection.

"Besides," she continued, "we army women feel that we are especially privileged, because we are making history, with our men, by keeping the home fires burning while the soldiers are guarding the railroad engineers and surveyors against the Indians as, mile by mile, in the face of almost insurmountable obstacles, they are building the railroads straight across the continent until the oceans meet, which will open up the country to civilization. Then the products of the Western grain and the wheat of Red River Valley, Dakota, said to be the richest in the world, will be conveyed to the Eastern and foreign markets. Mining properties will be developed, scientific farmers from all over the world will seek this virgin soil. Yes, my dear, we are the pioneer army women, and we're proud of it."

In the moment of silence that fell between us, I sensed her unspoken challenge and advice. "If

you have the courage, stay. If not, go. But be
sure of your decision."

Just then the clear voices of the sentinels drifting in from the outposts of the camp cut into the
still night with the reassuring call, "Two o'clock
—and all's well." Mrs. Custer sprang to her feet,
gave me a swift squeeze, and was out of the tent
in a jiffy.

What a soul-satisfying message that woman
brought to me! Next day, when I wrote home, I
knew my heart thoroughly.

By noon the following day our news had ceased
to be news, for not only we were too closely associ-
ated in our little community to keep anything
secret, but the rumor regarding the transfer of
the troops to Louisiana was verified in the mail
from Lincoln, which brought up the question of
my marriage. Should I go home for the event, or
should I be married at Lincoln as soon as the Black
Hills campaign was over? Mollie was strongly in
favor of the latter arrangement.

"Because," she argued, "most of the regiment
will be present then, and, after all, these people
are Frank's closest friends and will be yours. The
trip South will be your honeymoon, and we will
probably stop at Washington en route." But here
she spoiled everything by adding, "Besides, you'll
see practically nothing of your old friends from
now on, anyway."

For a moment my face and spirits fell, as I realized in truth that this frontier life exacted a toll
of social isolation. I suppose my expression regis-

tered pensiveness, for Mollie cut in impatiently, "You haven't heard a word I said."

"Oh, yes, I have," I hastened to correct her. "Go on."

Her plan was simple and practical. The troops would return to Lincoln on August 30, and, as Mollie had to pack her furniture and store it, preparatory to leaving with the regiment on September 29 for the Department of the Gulf, she proposed that the wedding take place that same day, as the troops immediately afterwards would scatter to their different stations.

The idea of such haste in railroading me into matrimony bewildered me, and my last shred of conventionality rose to protest.

"But what will Mother and Sister Sally say?" I wailed.

"Who cares?" retorted Mollie defiantly. "They have led shallow, sheltered lives, so you can't expect them to understand—at first—but they will after I've finished with them. You're lucky that you haven't Father to deal with, as I had."

I recalled that stormy scene when Mollie married Donald in deliberate defiance of our highstrung father, whose favorite slogan was, "A word and a blow," and who contended violently that the army and the plains were no fit settings for any man's daughter. It rocked the family harmony for quite a while, but everything calmed down ultimately, just as had the feud that existed between Mollie and our only brother. She gloried in the fact that she hadn't spoken to him for forty years, yet at the close of her life she remembered substantially in her will his only daughter, whom she had never seen.

But now we were occupied with my problem— only to Mollie it didn't exist. It seemed to her quite natural. The brevity of Frank's and my acquaintance she discounted, as she and Donald had known him intimately ever since he left his Philadelphia home when a mere boy to join the regiment as its youngest officer. Then, too, she understood the gamble with life out there and the uncertainty of it—so why not grasp every moment of happiness when it was offered? In fact, it was this hazard of existence that tempted adventurous souls and lured them into these regions. They lived and died with their boots on, scenting, seeking, finding danger — and they expected their women to stand by them.

Mollie's letter to our lady-mother went in the same mail as mine, so the die was cast. The plan met with Lieutenant Gibson's instant approval. Further, it was decided that, as he would have to rush back to Rice on August 31 to prepare for the Southern transfer, and would have no suitable accommodations for me, it might be wiser for me to remain with my family at Lincoln and help Mollie. There I would wait for us all to entrain together.

Our betrothal news was received with uproarious rejoicings. There were but few benedicts in the regiment then, and I was made so wholeheartedly welcome that it brought tears to my eyes.

"Tut tut," exclaimed the General. "Are you going to cry on me again?" This saved the situation and made me laugh.

Frank went around with his head in the clouds and bruises on his back from friendly pommeling.

It had been the habit of the younger officers to loaf, at nights, around a campfire—at a sufficient distance not to disturb the sleepyheads—and mull over the happenings of the day. Tonight, Frank had planned a little surprise and had wrangled some bacon, hardtack, and canned beans from the kitchen. The pork was pronged on long twigs and roasted, while the beans were shoved among the burning fagots.

Witty Lieutenant Weston was a prime favorite, but he had one bad defect. He loved his cot, and nothing could keep him out of it short of military duty. On this particular evening he made a beeline for his tent as usual. Frank called to him to join the crowd at the fire and be sociable, but he shook his head and went on.

"Aw, come on, John," wheedled Frank. "You won't die of exhaustion from one night's fun."

"Aw, come on," chorused the others.

But he remained adamant. They watched his candle flare and finally flicker out. They waited until he was thoroughly asleep, then Frank said with a chuckle, "Watch me get even with him." And he jumped to his feet.

He approached the tent and scratched on the fly.

"Who's there?" called the lieutenant sleepily.

Frank changed his voice and spoke with a

brogue. "The orderly, sir. Gineral Custer's compliments, and he wishes to see Lieutenant Weston at once."

Lieutenant Weston flopped disgustedly on his cot.

"Tell the General to go to Hell!" he ejaculated impatiently.

"All right, sir," said Frank, and he darted off, though the startled cry of "Orderly—come back!" rang in his ears.

Instantly the candle flared again, and those chuckling youngsters around the fire watched gleefully the tent shadow of a man jiggling frantically into a pair of trousers. In a few moments a tormented soul was hurrying toward the General's tent.

"Hello, John," exclaimed Frank, apparently surprised. "Thought you were in bed?"

"Was," came the retort, "but the General sent for me."

"Why?" queried Lieutenant Cook.

"Don't know." And a very much worried officer passed by. A few minutes later he returned.

"What did the General want?" asked Lieutenant Wallace.

"Oh, he——" and mumbling something under his breath, Weston fled to his own canvas.

Next morning on the firing range Frank felt John's eyes upon him. Finally the latter rode up beside him.

"So—you trifled with the truth—last night," he accused.

"Who, I?" demanded Frank, feigning innocence.

"Yes. The Gineral's orderly, hey?"

Frank chuckled. "And didn't I make a good one? What happened?"

"Well, when I got to Custer's tent it was totally dark. However, I scratched on the fly. He called out, 'Who's there?' 'Lieutenant Weston, sir,' I replied, beginning to feel a little screwy. 'Well, Lieutenant Weston, what do you want?' he asked. 'Why, nothing, sir,' I retorted, bewildered, 'but your orderly said you wanted to see me.' There was a pause, then the General suggested, 'I think you'd better see Lieutenant Gibson in the morning.' "

At this both victim and practical joker unloosed a volcano of heavy laughter which brought Lieutenant Weston's new and untried mount rearing on his hind feet. Incidentally, Mrs. Custer told me all about it, and we had much fun over it. In after years she used to say to me, wistfully, "You know, Katie, the memory of those little family intimacies in the regiment helps me to live over my army life."

The Buffalo Hunt

ix

THE REGIMENT was marching in five days, and last-minute preparations—the packing of added rations, supplies, ammunitions—were at fever heat. Yet the General and Tom staged a big surprise for our betrothal party.

When I first took up riding and shooting they promised me that if I qualified to their satisfaction they would permit me to witness (but not take part in) a buffalo hunt. As soon as Mrs. Custer told the General the news, at dawn next day a squad of soldiers were sent off on a mysterious errand. They located a herd of bison some miles away that were headed in the direction of camp, and a merry impromptu picnic was planned immediately.

Donald, who was a keen buffalo hunter, was denied this pleasure. The doctor wanted him to keep his leg in shape for the campaign, and this sort of sport required the hardest riding. Mollie and I, however, eager for everything, welcomed the idea gleefully. What fun and excitement beckoned! Soldiers were again sent out to keep the buffaloes in line and drive them slowly toward us.

Just at this time Captain Keogh and Lieutenant Edgerly, with a squad of enlisted men—all sta-

Captain Myles W. Keogh, killed at the Battle of the Little Bighorn. His horse, Comanche, was the only living thing found on the battlefield.

Lieutenant Winfield S. Edgerly, Seventh Cavalry, afterwards made General.

tioned at Fort Totten, Dakota Territory, and all
crack shots—joined us for a ten days' shooting
contest. Captain Keogh bunked in with Frank,
and, somehow, handsome Lieutenant Edgerly
wedged his six feet and four inches of length, huge
shoulders, and leonine head into the shared tent
of Lieutenants Varnum and Hodgson. Loud and
long were the good-natured grumblings that punctured the still nights thereafter, evoking sleepy
"Shut ups!" from adjacent canvas shelters. Everybody, however, eventually turned over in his
cot and snoozed again.

On the eve of the buffalo hunt, a coterie of us
was loitering in the moonlight outside of Donald's
and Mollie's tent, when Barney, Lieutenant Gibson's striker, stepped up to him, saluted, and said,
"Sorry, sir, but something's the matter with Blue
Streak."

Blue Streak was Frank's horse, which he had
been sparing, more or less, for the hunt, and the
remark awoke us to electric attention.

Immediately Frank joined the soldier and hurried off in the direction of the stables. An hour
later he returned, looking quite worried.

"How's Blue Streak?" queried Captain Keogh,
rolling a cigarette.

"Pretty sick," replied Frank. "Some fool fed
him an overdose of dried apples, and he's swollen
up like a poisoned pup. The vet's working over
him now."

"Why, who could have done such a thing?" exclaimed Mollie, who always had something to say.

"I bet a dollar Cuff did it," boomed Captain Keogh. "I'd beat the truth out of him, if I were you, Gib."

Cuff was a small negro waif to whom someone had once fed a decent meal. I always suspected Frank of being that culprit, because though the little darky promptly adhered to the regiment in true barnacle fashion—following it all over the plains—he concentrated a slavish devotion upon Lieutenant Gibson and all his belongings, and even began to dog *my* footsteps like a black poodle.

One day my investigating propensities impelled me to ask him a question. "Cuff, why are you so fond of Lieutenant Gibson?"

"I couldn't rightly say, Missy," he answered. "I jess likes him." Then he added: "Maybe 'cause my name's Frank, too."

"Really," I ejaculated, surprised. "Frank what?"

He hung his head, abashed. "I never did know my last name—reckon I never had none."

"But why do they call you Cuff?" I persisted.

He scratched his woolly pate. "Well, you see, I'se de general handy man 'bout here—fetches and carries most eberly thing, and—" he added proudly, "I'se de regiment masculot."

But to return to the absorbing question of the suffering Blue Streak. Captain Keogh was still talking.

"You say he denied it? He loves the horse?"

"Course he does," defended Frank.

"Hum," snorted the captain disgustedly. "Remember the time he fed him sour grass because he liked it?"

Frank smiled. "Yes, but he didn't mean to harm him." He paused. "However, I'm afraid my nag is out of commission for tomorrow."

Captain Keogh took a long drag on his cigarette. "Say, Gib, why don't you take my mount tomorrow? I'll be on the firing range all day and won't need him. You know how perfectly buffalo trained he is."

"Oh!" I cried eagerly. "That beautiful grey horse that looks as strong as granite? I'd like to ride him myself someday."

He snapped his glance down upon my small person, amused, and puffed wreaths of smoke. Then he smiled wryly. " 'Fraid not, young lady. Comanche is too mettlesome for a woman to handle. But you, Gib, take him—he has a yen for you anyway and your magic method of massaging his lower lip."

"Is that the reason he whinnies when he sees you, Frank?" I asked.

"Perhaps," he said, grinning. "Of course Blue Streak may be all right, but if not—why, thanks for your offer, Myles."

Next day Blue Streak was decidedly indisposed, so Frank rode big-boned, big-framed Comanche. Comanche, whose fame was to resound through the pages of history; Comanche, who, as much as any human being, was to play a dramatic role in the Indian activities of the Seventh Cavalry. Beneath a baking sun, upon the spot where there took

place that particular phase of the Battle of the
Little Bighorn—the Custer Massacre—that horse
was found, the only living thing on the still, desolate battlefield. There he had lain, riddled with
bullets, thousands of flies feasting upon his hide,
while above him circled hungry buzzards waiting
in grim patience for him to draw his last breath.
How tenderly the soldiers had lifted his suffering,
almost lifeless form; how gently, over rough,
uncharted terrain the government wagon had
directed its course: and how eagerly, anxiously,
every officer and enlisted man of the regiment
watched the gradual recovery of old Comanche,
the pet and trusted companion of a brave soldier,
a beloved and lost comrade, Captain Myles Keogh.

Well, the day of the hunt dawned bright and
clear, and everyone was up with the larks. We
packed our hampers with food, filled the canteens,
and dumped the whole into ambulance boots. The
conveyances also carried the women (Mollie and
I excepted, for we preferred our mounts) and
pulled out of camp. After proceeding several miles
we joined a detachment of mounted troopers, and
all waited for the word from our soldier scouts
to advance.

Expectancy pervaded all of us. The women,
though distinctly ordered to remain with the ambulance, were armed with powerful field glasses with
which they hoped to find a hilltop within range of
the hunt.

Carbines flashed in the sun, spurs jangled,
horses whinnied and pawed the ground, for they

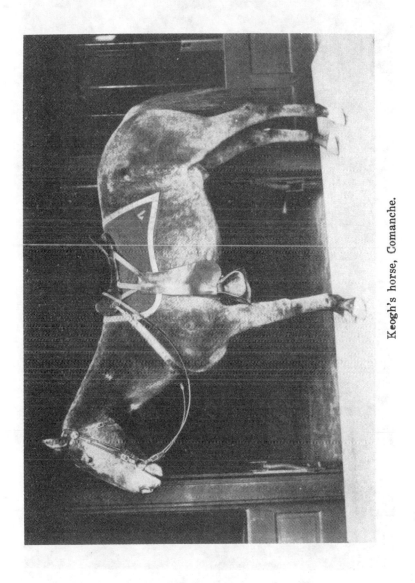

Keogh's horse, Comanche.

MRS. DONALD MCINTOSH

knew all about it. These equines had been trained in this particular sport, just as fast ponies are taught polo, and they fairly itched to be off. Everyone, including the women, carried a revolver.

General Custer wore a blue flannel shirt, loosened at the throat, a daring red tie, buckskin trousers stuffed into troop boots, a cartridge belt, and he carried a carbine and two revolvers. The others were clad similarly, but were minus ties and wore old uniform trousers. One and all donned tight-fitting caps or handkerchiefs tied about their heads to break the force of the air while speeding. Lieutenant Gibson looked singularly handsome in a navy blue bandanna scarf.

"All you need now is a pair of hoop earrings to proclaim you a gypsy king," I said laughingly.

"It might not be a bad life at that," he declared. "I seem to feel the virus of it seeping through my veins already."

It seemed that word would never come. Then suddenly two horsemen, who proved to be our own soldier scouts, were sighted riding rapidly over the hill. The herd had been driven within a few miles of us, and immediately the hunters leaped away. The excitement injected itself into the mules, for they broke into a gallop, raking the ambulances and swinging them drunkenly from side to side, until the drivers could bring them under control. Mollie and I followed the others at a fast gallop, and in a short time we reached the hunting ground.

To the human eye, watching these slowly moving

herds from a distance, the scene pictured was prosaically pastoral. In fact, these prairie rovers rarely showed viciousness unless attacked, preferring to lumber along peacefully in their bovine way. But, like the stalking of all wild animals, they had to be approached from leeward to avoid the warning of human scent, and, safe on the opposite hill, we breathlessly watched our men deploy. In a jiffy the ambulances were emptied of their female cargo, and, armed with field glasses, Mrs. Custer, Maggie Calhoun, Mrs. McDougall, Annie Yates, and others viewed the animated panorama with tense interest. But Mollie and I, on fast horses, paralleled the hunters on the opposite hill.

They approached the herd cautiously and were creeping closer to them, when something, perhaps the rustle of grasses or the dull thud of horses' hoofs on the spongy sod, must have reached the acute ears of the beasts, for suddenly the whole herd, calves and all, were tearing off at an amazing speed—amazing, because these animals weighed from seven to nine hundred pounds. Now the horses jumped to the fore, their legs stretched so wide that their bellies seemed almost to touch the ground, while their riders lay flat against their flanks and necks. What a race! Mollie and I, carried away by the excitement, found ourselves pounding along on our own hill, still paralleling them. The horses were now hedging the buffaloes, in order to keep them from separating and running amuck. Never had I viewed anything so thrilling, as Mollie and I literally flew along, still keeping in line with the hunt. Finally we reached a smaller hill, where we paused to draw breath while we glued our eyes upon the thundering herd and listened to the sharp reports of the carbines and revolvers.

And then two things occurred. As we started again Mollie's horse abruptly went lame. "Stone," she called to me against the wind and slid to the ground, where she picked up a sharp twig, lifted each hoof of the animal, and scanned it closely. At that moment I glimpsed the herd plunging down the sides of the plateau, where it was almost swallowed up in the high grasses. To the naked eye distances are difficult to compute on the plains because of atmospheric conditions. Hence, when a great beast with short, bristling mane and matted coat suddenly appeared, seemingly from nowhere, my sense of space proportions went blank. The creature must have been nearer to us than we imagined, or he had strayed from the herd.

I was slightly out of his range, but Mollie and her horse loomed straight ahead of him. Terror locked my voice and body as the unsuspecting woman bent leisurely over her task of dislodging the stone in her horse's hoof. My own mount, at a safe distance from the bison, had stretched the reins from my listless fingers sufficiently far to enable him to nibble the grass. How long my nightmare might have lasted is problematical, but, at sight of the kneeling woman, the buffalo stopped briefly in astonishment, and, strangely enough, this action snapped me out of my lethargy. Instantly every sense jumped as though pricked by a needle, and certain facts dinned into me by Tom Custer and the General flooded my mind. The skull of a bison is impervious to bullets. He must be shot under the left foreleg. This meant perilous proximity to the beast, but, thank God, I had never missed one day's shooting, rain or shine, and I could try. I didn't warn Mollie, because, if I drew the attention of the bison to myself, he would switch his position and throw me out of range for my shot. Besides, she was too hopelessly out of line herself and could never mount and get away on a lame horse anyway. I can well credit the reputed mental pictures of drowning people, for within the space of a few seconds an infinitude of past, fantastic details swept through my brain. Then I came to, alert, tingling with the frantic realization of Mollie's peril.

The beast was recovering from his bewilderment. His tail flicked uneasily, and the shaggy head, hanging between massive shoulders, started to shake angrily, while his flat mane rose in bristles. Instantly I jerked my gun from its holster, yanked my horse's head from the grass, and dug my spurs into his flanks. He sprang away, panting, and we reached the buffalo just as he was swinging into preliminary speed before he charged.

Mollie was still some distance away. Closer and closer I drew to the fetid-smelling fur, but could not take aim as we were going so fast. And then Mollie, still intent on her job, unconsciously helped me.

"There!" she shrilled loudly, exultantly. "It's out."

The sound of this voice again arrested the buffalo. He faltered. Caution and cunning held him for a few seconds, and here I seized my chance. Leaning way over in my saddle, I aimed for his left foreleg and shot—once — twice. The beast whirled upon me, so close that I could almost feel the breath of his fiery nostrils, and plunged. My horse, untrained for bison hunting, shied violently and, leaping to one side, threw me to the ground, where I lay holding a smoking revolver. I must have lost consciousness, because, when I opened my eyes, Mollie, chalky white, was bending over me, trying to force some liquor between my lips. Frank, too, was kneeling beside me on the grass, his olive skin blanched beneath his tan, his dark eyes wide with anxiety.

I blinked groggily, for the picture was unreal, of course, because he had dashed off with the hunting party, and Mollie—— Here recollection came stabbing through my brain, and I sat up trembling.

"Oh, Mollie!" I exclaimed hysterically, clinging to her. "You're—you're safe!"

For once in her life words failed her, but she strained me to her so tensely that I could feel her heart pounding against my own.

Here Frank broke in.

"Are you all right?" he murmured huskily.

"Oh, yes," I quavered, trying to smile. "Just a bit shaky."

"Let's see," he said, and raised me carefully from the ground. "Now—walk."

I took a few steps, somewhat wobbily, but without pain. He and Mollie heaved sighs of relief. I leaned against her and glanced about investigatingly. There on the ground, only a few yards away, sprawled the buffalo. After the bullet, or bullets, went home, he evidently had had sufficient impetus left to charge in the direction where I would have been, but for the blessed shying of my horse; and then he had dropped dead.

Lieutenant Hare, a big, rangy Texan, who had ridden practically from his cradle, was examining the carcass. Again I marveled, because he, too, had been one of the hunting group. Suddenly I missed Frank and shifted my gaze. I caught my breath, for there he stood beside General Custer, who was dismounted and holding the reins of Dandy and Comanche. Strangely enough, they were regarding me sternly. Confused, I looked askance from one to the other. Frank had been so solicitous for me a few minutes before, but now his eyes had hardened.

"You were told to remain with the rest of the women," he accused, in the cold, impersonal tone that he used with the soldiers.

I stared at him with incredulous eyes, bewildered. He was like a total stranger. "Why—I didn't realize——" I stammered, looking hopefully toward the General. But this time he failed me, and his keen blue eyes surveyed me stonily. He moved away toward Lieutenant Hare, who was still looking over my "kill."

But here Mollie found her voice in a rush. "You know it wasn't done purposely," she flared.

"Silence!" commanded Frank, his voice cutting like metal. "You're to blame more than she is."

Astonished, she was bridling to reply, when a soldier appeared leading my horse, which had bolted after he threw me.

"Come, Katie," said my sister, acidly. "We're leaving." Then she called to Lieutenant Hare. "Oh, Mr. Hare, may I have my horse, please?"

The officer looked up from the dead buffalo. He had the reins of Mollie's mount flung over his arm, along with his own. His silent attitude also reflected distinct disapproval.

By now my bewilderment was being drowned in wrath, and, as Frank approached to help me mount, I suddenly picked up my riding-habit skirt, whirled, and marched straight toward the General and the dead bison. As violence seemed to be the order of the day, I might as well see what I had slain.

The General rose from his knees as I stood beside him.

"I—I hate him!" I exploded under my breath.

"You don't," he contradicted flatly. "You little fool, you deliberately disobeyed instructions issued for your own safety and his peace of mind, and you deserved what you got." Then he added, less tempestuously, "You know you shouldn't have done it, but—" he pointed to the beast— "Holy Mackerel, am I proud of your marksmanship!"

Somewhat mollified, I smiled. I looked over my shoulder and saw Frank standing alone beside my horse, patiently waiting for me.

The soldier who had brought my horse, at a sign from the General came hurrying toward the buffalo, where they evidently discussed what was to be done with it. Mollie was already in her saddle, Lieutenant Hare in his, and they were busy talking. I meandered slowly to where I belonged, my mind mulling over things, for though this whole affair had not really been my fault, yet there were phases of it that required consideration. When I reached Frank I suddenly stopped and, standing on tiptoe, lifted my face and shyly saluted the end of his chin, the only spot my small stature could attain. He grinned boyishly. I smiled foolishly, our horses nosed each other companionably, and the General swung into his saddle, waved his hand, and dashed away to rejoin the hunt.

It seemed that Mollie's and my spurt along the opposite hill had not been noted, as all eyes had been glued upon the buffaloes. But when the stray animal tore away from the herd and headed in our direction, Lieutenant Hare had happened to look up and saw two moving specks, which a hasty glance through field glasses revealed to be women riding headlong into the path of the creature. He had yelled to Frank and the General, who were a few feet ahead of him, and the three of them had plunged after the beast, which by this time had

outstripped them considerably, and they had arrived just in time to see me dispatch him.

Well, my hunting feat was a nine-hour wonder,
and my victim, with the rest of the kill, provided
an ample meal for the entire command.

From then on, our men became practically invisible from dawn to tattoo, so much had to be
done before the big push into the Black Hills.
Added to these hectic hours, the expedition was
joined by a well-equipped scientific party, which
resulted in much valuable information pertaining
to geology, zoology, and paleontology being gathered in the regions explored, although the presence
of precious metal in large quantities was doubted.
General Custer, however, reported that gold had
been found in the "grass roots," creating newspaper furor, criticisms, and controversy.

Preparations proceeded with lightning celerity.
Nothing was overlooked, for daily reports of each
march had to be recorded. Small pen-and-ink
maps, that marked the locations of streams, and
regimental encampments for the night, had to be
made. Fords, rolling prairies, high ridges, level
plains, and the Pacific Railroad lines (then under
construction) had to be indicated. The minutiae
of the whole adventure seemed never ending.

Fort Rice

x

ON JULY 2, at 4:20 A.M., reveille sounded as the dawn mist beaded the grass, cactus, and sagebushes. Within two hours, not a horse, man, or piece of equipment was left on the silent prairie, for the campaign had begun.

The breaking of camp was accomplished with such swift military precision that to an outsider, like myself, it seemed not only bewildering, but unreal. The early rising, the spasmodic combing of one's hair by the crazily swinging mirror, the hastily swallowed breakfast of hardtack, bacon, and coffee—all these contributed to a kind of queer dream.

Two soldiers waited outside each tent until the meal was over, and, at a given signal, each canvas was leveled to the ground at the same moment, and then rolled up and stowed away in government covered wagons. Every article of tent furnishing was disposed of in similar fashion.

When I saw what was happening I gasped in dismay and ran to my own tent. I recalled several pieces of apparel that had been flung on the cot or pinned, wet after rinsing, on the canvas to dry. These I snatched up, and, lifting the lid of my trunk, threw them in and sat on the top. Even so, a few underthings, very much laced, had been whisked away by the eternally blowing wind and had alighted on the grass or got snarled in a cactus bush, where they either played hide and seek with sundry scraps of paper, fluttering blithely on the plain, or were torn by thorns. These I had to sprint after, finally returning triumphant, but embarrassed. However, no one heeded me, for I was soon to learn that the speed in making or breaking camp was a regimental vanity, and nothing else mattered for the moment. In fact, during the whole campaign these processes of military figuring didn't vary more than five minutes, according to regimental record.

Seasoned army women accepted the whole procedure with the utmost calm, but, when the entire command was ready to move and "Boots and Saddles" sounded and the column as one man vaulted into their saddles, I quivered with excitement, and when they marched away with the band blaring, "The Girl I Left Behind Me," I twisted my handkerchief miserably, despite the fact that Lieutenant Gibson rode up to me at the last moment, calling gaily, "Don't forget. I'll be back in sixty days, and then——" His horse plunged once in the air, and they were gone.

But would he be back? In panic I turned to Mollie. "Will—will anything happen to him?"

"Not likely," she replied, "but you never can tell. That's what we army women are confronted with—*uncertainty.*" And that was all the consolation I got out of her. Mrs. Custer and Maggie Calhoun accompanied the column part of the way but returned to Fort Lincoln the next day, escorted by the paymaster.

The desolate camp seemed like a silent mystery raft, and the boundless June green prairies a mighty ocean upon which we were launched, time and port unknown, and I stared dreamily at our belongings standing out starkly on the empty plain. However, the few unimaginative soldiers left to police the place cut short my reverie as they heaved trunks and boxes into several government trucks; the women, meanwhile, piled briskly into ambulances which were to take them back to the garrison.

There was much to be done during those sixty intervening days, as far as I was concerned—letters to write, a wedding dress to be made as soon as the material arrived from the East. Wonderful, nuptial decorations, in bright-colored bunting, were planned to give the quarters a festive air, for a simple reception was to follow the ceremony.

Mollie had insisted that we make a week's visit to Mrs. Benteen at Fort Rice, not only because she had promised her, but she wanted me to meet the wife of Frank's troop commander. So we no sooner returned to Lincoln than we were en route across country for Rice. The officer in command at Lincoln kindly offered us the use of an ambulance, and we started off, leaving "Rise" to keep house until our return.

It was a blistering day, Dakota's climatic freakishness running true to form, for the night before we had slept under blankets. During the spring, floods menaced lives, swamped ranches, washed away cattle sheds; then would follow such spells of burning dryness that the earth cracked, seeds shriveled in the ground, dust storms swept the prairies, and heat, which flickered before your eyes, would assail plants, man, and beast like the thongs of a red-hot whip.

I regretted wasting a whole week of priceless time at Rice, because there were so many little details attendant upon a home wedding. Still, as Mollie pointed out, I had practically nothing to buy of importance, for my wardrobe fitted admirably into the Southern honeymoon picture, so I had to accept her decision gracefully.

Besides the ambulance driver, another soldier, fully armed, was detailed to escort us on our trip, for one never knew what might be encountered in the offing. Perhaps a stray, irate buffalo, or maybe the remote possibility of a hostile or two turning up to make things unpleasant. Anyway, we were taking no chances. As it was, we were momentarily startled from time to time by bronzed figures, clothed in breechcloths, rising suddenly from behind large sagebrushes or other bushes. However, they simply stared at us in their usual sullen manner, their moccasins puffing out spurts of dust as they mushed along in the direction of small hills where their ponies were trying to extract a bit of sustenance from the bone-dry, crackling grasses.

By this time I was getting used to the back-breaking rides, up and down gullies and across

seemingly endless spaces, while the sun baked
down upon the ambulance with a heat that was
almost enough to ignite our trunk, strapped on
top. An unprecedented plague of grasshoppers
flooded the land—huge armies of them which destroyed the crops and leaped up into our faces, or
slid to the floor where they bunched themselves into green mattresses. They were everywhere, and
the frenzied mules tossed their heads violently,
trying to dislodge the pests from their ears.

Finally weathering the alkali dust, heat, and
insects, we reached Fort Rice, one of the most Godforsaken spots on earth.

I saw a stockade post, located on the upper banks
of the Missouri River, which, garrisoned by a few
troops of cavalry and companies of infantry, was
the sole protection for miles around of the few
pioneers and their scattered ranches against
hordes of Indians who trekked back and forth from
their reservation at Standing Rock, situated some
sixty miles below. Desolation marked this country
as its own. It wailed from every blade of scorched,
brittle grass; it trickled from every drop of cloudy
liquid, called, by courtesy, water. It sobbed into
the barren earth as a childless woman protests to
Mother Nature. Atop the steaming bastions, soldier sentinels, sweat rolling down their faces and
bouncing upon their swollen, mosquito-bitten
hands, kept alert eyes upon the bare, dreary
horizon.

At our approach, however, those hands that
were eternally clutching the carbines brought their

butts to the ground with a thud and permitted us
to enter the garrison proper. Flanked on one side
of the sun-baked parade ground, rickety frame
houses designated as officers' quarters confronted
us, while across the plains soldiers' barracks
loomed forlornly.

Lincoln was by no means a dream of luxury,
but this post, soon to be abandoned, seemed like
the conception of some nightmare; yet two years
later I could have knelt and kissed its very dust
in gratitude for what it did for me.

Mrs. Benteen, with one child in her arms and
another dragging at her skirts, came down the
steps to welcome us. She was tall and thin, the
antithesis of her stocky, handsome husband. She
greeted us with flattering cordiality. She and
Mollie were evidently very intimate, for, at sight,
of the latter, young Fred rushed up to her and
hugged her heartily. He eyed me suspiciously.

"Who's she?" he asked.

"My sister."

"Is she married?"

"Not yet," she assured him, "but she will be
soon. And what do you think? She's going to join
our regiment."

That seemed to satisfy him, for he sank upon
the rotting old floor where he played "cattle roundup" with lots of marbles.

Mollie and Mrs. Benteen plunged at once into
regimental gossip, which left me free to look
around. Such a place! It was sparsely furnished,
as all other garrison quarters, but where it had

been papered with newspapers to keep the cold in winter and the heat in summer out of the yawning crevices, there were spaces of cottonwood planks left bare. Here the children had torn off strips of the ancient journals, giving the walls a queer kind of appearance.

By this time I was used to canned food, but I had to struggle to survive the concentrated fury of the millions of mosquitoes, so tiny that they slipped through the finest netting. Yet, despite this discomfort, I really enjoyed myself. Of course, I was among Frank's friends, which helped a lot, and I was wont to sit by the hour at the feet of these older women and drink in every word they said about him, from his pranks to his more serious side. One anecdote that was rather amusing had to do with the arrival at the post of a new youngster, one night, too late for duty.

Frank happened to be the first officer he met, so he eagerly questioned him about many things, especially the personality of General Custer, then in command.

"Oh," said Frank, "he's a strict disciplinarian, but a fine man. He has, however, one defect: he's hard of hearing and very sensitive about it. So be careful to raise your voice when you meet him."

The grateful boy was profuse in his thanks for the advice, and turned in early.

Later that night Frank dropped in at the Custers' and mentioned that he had met the new man. The General was smearing cheese on hardtack, and looked up quickly.

"Like him?" he inquired in his jerky way.

"Very much," returned Frank, "but it's too bad he's a trifle deaf."

"Deaf?" echoed the General. "Why, he's just out of the Point."

Frank shrugged, adding by way of explanation, "I believe his uncle is something of a politician. Anyway, the poor chap's sensitive about it, so I raised my voice in speaking to him."

"Hum!" grunted the General, shoving the cheese across the table. "Help yourself."

Well, the next day, when the officer reported for duty, both men began to bawl at each other. The conversation became so noisy that soldiers strolling about pricked up their ears, while Frank and a bunch of youngsters in on the joke were doubled up with laughter just outside the adjutant's office, as they listened to the strident duologue.

Finally the General demanded, "Why are you screaming at me?"

"But you're shouting at me, sir."

"But you're supposed to be deaf," defended the elder officer.

"And so are you, sir."

There was a sudden hush, and the culprit and his gang sneaked away just as the General said in lowered tones, "When you see Lieutenant Gibson, tell him to report to me."

"And what did he do to Frank?" I asked anxiously.

But Mrs. Benteen only bit a thread and shook her head. "Nothing very startling, I imagine, as

Gibby was back that night to help finish the cheese."

Then she went on reminiscing. One evening in Kansas City the General and Lieutenant Gibson decided to take in a one-night show, sponsored by a third-rate stock company. The unpainted, frame, ramshackle building, termed a theater, was lighted by kerosene lamps, but despite its crudities and atrocious performance, the officers could obtain only rail seats in the balcony. Soon the boresome play, coupled with the fumes of dimly turned down lamps, stale tobacco, and odors emanating from the chaps of ranchmen and cowboys, lent an atmosphere of drowsy closeness to the place, and Frank began to yawn. Rousing himself, he peered over the railing into the orchestra, and directly beneath him he spied a huge ranchman, his head as bare as a billiard ball, who was sniveling into a purple handkerchief, as a frowsy, whiskey-voiced female on the stage wailed about a dying mother. Sitting in semiobscurity in an end seat, the lieutenant slid a program from a pile lying on the steps beside him, crumpled it, and took aim for the inviting pate. Missed it—again and again—because the target would not stay still.

Custer, noting the poor marksmanship, whispered, "Slip me a couple."

Frank handed him half the pile, and, hitching themselves forward over the railing, they bombarded the emotional one—but in vain, for the shiny head kept bobbing and wagging with every nose blast. So intent were the conspirators in their task they forgot everything else, until, suddenly glancing up, Frank discovered that every eye in the balcony was focused on them.

Quickly he nudged the General, who, taking in the scene with a glance, mumbled, "Let's duck," and as they tiptoed out of their seats the rafters roared with laughter.

So much for Frank's pranks. But Mrs. de Rudio gave me another slant to his character while we cut and basted clothes for her little brood of four.

Shortly after he joined the regiment at Fort Riley, Kansas, he was ordered to the Cavalry School at Fort Leavenworth. The ambulance which took him there carried one other passenger, the wife of an enlisted man, en route to the town of Leavenworth.

The day, as usual, was insufferably hot, the springless conveyance bumping and bouncing in and out of holes and wagon trails, and, as they progressed thus violently, the officer noted from time to time that the woman would bite her lips, while beads of perspiration stood out upon her brow.

Again and again he offered her his canteen of water, which she accepted gratefully. Suddenly, when they were miles away from any habitation, a little blue pond sprang up just ahead of them, and then the woman spoke.

Said she, white-lipped, "I'm sorry, sir, but you'll have to stop the ambulance, for I'm going to have —a child."

Child? No sudden report from a rifle could

have astounded the young man more, but after a few seconds he controlled himself and ordered the driver to draw up as close as possible to the pond. Then the two men spread gunny sacks from the boot on the grass, upon which they placed the suffering woman. Water, a few handkerchiefs, and a penknife had to serve as surgical instruments. Then, following instructions from the patient, the young lieutenant did his best, and finally, beneath a blazing sun, a wee, very premature recruit blinked his unseeing eyes and sent forth a wail upon the silent prairies.

Quickly the officer and driver drew the curtains of the ambulance and shut out the glare of the sun, spread a few more gunny sacks in the bottom, where they gently laid the woman, then Lieutenant Gibson, slipping out of his uniform blouse, wrapped the baby in it, perched his forage cap over the infant's head to protect the little eyes, and carried him to his mother. After that he leaped up beside the driver, the whip cracked sharply, and the old ambulance creaked slowly toward Leavenworth.

"Oh," I breathed, lifting anxious eyes to Mrs. de Rudio, "and did the baby live?"

"Yes, indeed," she laughed, "in spite of his four and a half pounds." Then, more seriously, she added, "Gibby did that, and he just a boy himself, so to speak."

And my own heart swelled with pride in my man.

A ball was to be given at Bismarck, and Mollie was asked to chaperone the young people going from Rice. An ambulance was to take us and bring us back, and we set forth one morning with the temperature high enough to cook an egg. The crusted soil saw its infant corn parch in its husks and its wheat curl up and gladly die. However, these pleasure-loving youngsters permitted no such trifles to interfere with their holiday, so we jogged along merrily until we reached the Little Heart River. This stream, though not long, was of great depth and had to be approached from a steep incline. Here we paused to look around and dislodge a flock of horseflies as big as wasps that kept company with the tiny, nipping mosquitoes, both of which were irritating the mules.

As we glanced across the river we saw a narrow bridge spanning it, hardly wide enough to accommodate two vehicles at the same time. A ranchman had stopped his team of horses right in the middle of it to water the animals, though why he couldn't have waited until he reached the other side will always remain a mystery.

Mollie took one look at the outlay, then stated, "You people may do as you please, but I propose to get out with my sister and walk across that bridge."

Our driver was getting ready to cross, and a chorus of protests arose.

"Why, how silly! Why cook yourself to death unnecessarily?" But Mollie was adamant.

Already the ambulance wheels were turning, but she called to the driver peremptorily, "Stop this ambulance, driver."

The soldier hesitated, then halted his mules, and she and I got out, I feeling like a perfect fool but not wanting to make a scene. The driver looked to the officers for further orders, but, though the men grumbled and the women were peevish, they, too, finally decided to get out.

More horseflies swarmed over the tormented mules, and, as the driver leaned back, applying his foot to the brakes, the beasts tossed their heads restively. They started downhill and in a few minutes were on the bridge, the animals becoming more and more irritable. However, they dragged the ambulance across the wooden planks, and all went well until they met the team of horses. These poor creatures, their noses plunged into pails, were also lashing their tails against the maddening hordes of insects.

The ambulance was now abreast of them, the margin for passing being but a few inches, then a mule lunged against a horse, and instantly pandemonium was let loose. Mules and horses reared, harnesses became entangled, the creatures kicked and bit at each other viciously, and, before our eyes, the rotting old structure began to sway slightly, then more and more, as the frenzied animals tried to extricate themselves from the harnesses and bolt. From swaying, the bridge started to rock, and finally, with a terrific crash, the timbers gave way, splitting the whole thing in the middle, and horses, mules, ranchman, and soldier were plunged into the depths below, where both had their brains kicked out, and the animals, dragging the heavy vehicle after them, were borne to the bottom.

For a moment we were all too stunned to speak, then Zoe Godfrey rushed convulsively into Mollie's arms.

"Oh, Mrs. Mac," she sobbed, "you've saved our lives!"

The men were silent. The rest of us sank on the plain in collapse. Finally, Lieutenant Ogle, of the infantry, spoke, "We will find some sort of conveyance for you women, but we must remain here to recover the bodies."

This assurance of our return to Rice, combined with the gratitude we felt for our miraculous escape, did much to calm us and fortify us for the long wait we would have to endure under the baking sun before we could procure transportation. At last, however, escorted by another officer, we began our subdued return trip.

In the early morning hours Mrs. Benteen, who was sitting in her window unable to sleep, heard the far-off rumble of some sort of rig, and as the noise became louder she finally realized that whatever it was must be stopping at her door. A hastily lighted candle revealed that her guests of the day before were returning in a ranchman's hayrick.

A day or two later the other two officers returned with the soldier's body, which was laid to rest in the little cemetery outside the stockade, shared by Indians and white men alike.

Thus I met my first army tragedy and the loss of a prized evening gown, as our luggage, of

course, went down with the wreck; yet, sobering
as the experience had been, I still enjoyed my visit
to desolate old Fort Rice, and here, too, during
those days when time was quickly bridged, I made
firm friendships.

Every morning I spent on the different porches,
learning more and more of the regiment I was so
soon to join. Once I asked of sweet, frail Mrs.
Godfrey the reason that Lieutenant Godfrey called
my Frank, "George."

"Because," she replied, "Edwin is devoted to
Gibby, and his favorite name is George."

"But," I countered, "your son's name is Guy."

"Yes," she nodded, "I insisted upon calling him
after Guy Mannering. I liked that book; but I
realize now that Edwin was disappointed."

Back to Fort Abraham Lincoln

xi

FINALLY our visit ended. Owing to the bridge collapse, we had to be rowed across the Little Heart River. That same day, Lieutenant Ogle of the infantry was taking an insane soldier to Bismarck with an extra soldier for guard, and the three of them accompanied us. The maniac was a huge creature, and every few minutes he kept jumping up in that small boat and rocking it with his weight until the sides nearly paralleled the water. If it had capsized we would all have been drowned, for neither Mollie nor I could swim, and the men would have been too busy saving their prisoner. Fortunately, the latter was not dangerous, but every now and then he would ask, "Do you know my brother-in-law Jones?" Of course, we shook our heads, then he would continue. "He's a terrible man. He won't let me sleep, but keeps loosening thousands of snails on my bed." And this conversation went on over and over again.

We found an ambulance from Lincoln awaiting us on the other side, and all five of us piled into it, the prisoner sitting opposite to us, handcuffed between the officer and his brawny guard.

What a day we experienced, with the madman suddenly deciding that Mollie was his sister Jennie, and pleading with her not to let her husband persecute him with snails. This and the heat and the grasshoppers made the trip fantastic.

For several months there had not been a drop of rain, and, except for the heavy dews, the plains would have become arid deserts. However, now, as much to break the strained silence as anything else, I remarked to Mollie, "Oh, look at that tiny green cloud over there."

A startled expression leaped into her eyes. "Where?" she asked quickly.

"Where?" echoed Lieutenant Ogle uneasily. Then the officer said briskly to the soldier guard, indicating the prisoner, "You can hold him, while I help the driver."

He halted the ambulance, unshackled himself from the madman, and got out. The green patch already was becoming perceptibly larger, and a light wind was springing up.

"It looks as though we might have a little rain," I observed.

"A little rain?" echoed Mollie. "It means both rain and hail and plenty of it."

The officer and driver were feverishly placing huge stones under the wheels of the ambulance to steady it; they also got robes and newspapers from the boot and shoved them through the windows for extra covering.

Rapidly the cloud flung widening green tentacles across the sky, which reflected their bilious hue upon the earth, and suddenly the quickening breeze was throttled, leaving the air dead, as if a vacuum had sucked up all animation. Pending this breathless lull, the brittle grasses rattled, as hundreds of frightened, wild things darted through them and scuttled for refuge into holes or under strong bushes.

With the first flash of lightning, followed by distant thunder, the mules lifted their heads uneasily and sniffed the air like dogs. And now the prisoner stood erect, almost jerking his guard off the seat, and lunged for the door. Instantly his powerful bodyguard dragged him back, trying to calm him, but in vain, and a scuffle ensued. Then Mollie rose and took Lieutenant Ogle's seat. Very quietly she reached out and touched the madman on the arm. "Jennie's here," she stated, and with that he relaxed like a tired child and sank on the seat beside her.

I stared at her with frightened eyes and quickening heart, wondering what would happen when he realized that he had been fooled, but he turned to her and smiled vacantly.

"Oh, Jennie," he mumbled, "you've come to save me from the snails."

Mollie nodded and, taking the man's big paw in one of her small, white hands, held it soothingly. It was just as simple as that, and I crossed my fingers to keep him in that mood.

The wind was picking up again; the storm, with increasing thunder and lightning was almost upon us.

With a last cleating down of the canvas curtains, Lieutenant Ogle sprang into the stage. He started when he saw Mollie nursing the maniac and of-

fered to relieve her, but she shook her head warn-
ingly. The poor fellow was, at least, calm. The
driver also joined us, which impelled me to ask
anxiously, "What have you done with the mules?
They might run away."

"They have run away," answered Lieutenant
Ogle. "We had to free them or have the ambulance
capsized, so they're on their way back to Lincoln
by this time."

Fortunately, we were not far from the garrison.
Yet, facing the night on the empty prairie, with
only a few sandwiches left from lunch, was far
from alluring, but I looked into those stoic faces
and forced myself to be calm.

The storm broke. Thunder and lightning split
the air, and the noise was like a terrific explosion.
The wind screamed, ploughed up the soil, and
rocked our old stage. Down came the rain, as
heavy as spilled-over oceans. It was mixed with
hail as large as hen's eggs. I had seen something
of this phenomenon from the train window under
shelter, but this private exhibit, with nothing between me and the actual elements except a bit of
canvas, was quite different, and I found myself
clinging frantically to Lieutenant Ogle's brass
buttons until every one of them was wrenched off.

A flood of rain seeped through the curtains,
soaking the floor of the ambulance, while hail
pounded the top, slit the canvas, and often bounced
into our very laps. Yet, through it all, the madman, thinking his sister was beside him and pro-
tecting him, remained unruffled.

When the storm had spent itself we looked out upon a plain robbed of its topsoil and pitted and pockmarked by hail. The temperature had dropped many degrees, and a cold moon hung amidst a setting of bleached-out stars.

We divided our sparse fare, the sandwiches and one remaining can of beans, and prepared for the night, using a few old newspapers for covering, as our robes were soaking wet. The officer and driver insisted upon removing their blouses and giving them to Mollie and me. Mollie never relinquished her vigil over her afflicted charge, who slept fitfully.

Thus we spent the night—six of us, hungry and alone, adrift upon seemingly endless space. The moonlight cast shadows of drooping-tailed coyotes, as the creatures slunk across the plain; otherwise all was as silent as a dead world. Our three responsible men slept soundly, but Mollie and I only dozed, being wide-awake and chilled to the bone at the first sweet notes of the early-rising meadow lark. Out of the grey glow heralding the birth of a new day, all nature began to stir, from crawling things to skipping rabbits and scratching prairie hens.

Fanlike rays of light slowly turned the horizon to amber; then the sun rose in flaming glory, bathing these lonely spaces in lavish, vivid beauty. As I gazed in rapt wonder at it all, I saw some dark specks looming on the brow of the hill, and instantly I became possessive. Who or what were these interlopers, daring to intrude upon our pri-

vate plain? As I continued to look, my indignation
gave place to a feeling of uneasiness. Suppose they
were Indians? The red man was always a question, whether friendly or hostile, and here I roused
the other occupants of the ambulance. They were
instantly awake.

Immediately the insane soldier became a problem. He clamored for a breakfast that didn't exist.
The rest of us, minus field glasses, focused our
anxious eyes upon the enlarging specks. It wasn't
until a friendly "Hello" drifted to us across the
plain that we heaved sighs of relief. Prairie-
trained horses, carefully avoiding holes, cautiously
picked their way through buffalo grass and under-
brush. Mounted upon them we discerned a woman
in riding habit and wide-brimmed hat, beside
whom rode a man in civilian's clothes. Then came
two more mounted women and, last, an army ambulance. A shout of welcome burst from us as we
recognized Elizabeth Custer, the contract doctor,
Maggie Calhoun, and Mrs. McDougall.

The arrival of our unharnessed mules the night
before alarmed the garrison, and immediately
Mrs. Custer organized a rescue party, bringing
food, medical supplies, some guns and ammunition,
and four fresh mules, in case our ambulance could
be hauled. Knowing our route from Rice, they had
no difficulty in tracing us, but those sturdy souls
rode all night to reach us as soon as possible. Of
course, they were greatly relieved to find us none
the worse for the wear, and the soldiers built a
fire, rifled the ambulance of food supplies, and in

a jiffy we were enjoying one of the grandest break-
fasts ever set before mortal eyes.

By now fluffy, pearl-white clouds, shaped like
swans, their heads tucked under their wings,
floated in the sky, which was a symphony of color.

The doctor promptly took the befuddled man in
charge, accompanying him in our old stage with
Lieutenant Ogle and the soldier guard.

Then Mollie and I insisted that the tired
women get into the other ambulance while we
rode their mounts, and thus, with body and mind
refreshed, on a day radiating sunshine and happiness, we journeyed back to Fort Lincoln, the
anxious ordeal over.

What a joy to reach Headquarters again! After
Rice it seemed the quintessence of luxury and
comfort, and surprises awaited us. First there
were letters from Frank and Donald, one from
my lady-mother, also another from my elder sister, and then there were two more—one from my
mother to Frank, and one from Frank's mother
to me.

My letter from mother was very tender and a
bit wistful, because the West seemed appallingly
far away and she was growing older. However, it
was my happiness that counted. Sister Sally's
missive ran somewhat along the same lines, not
failing, however, to stress the briefness of Frank's
and my acquaintance, that she hoped our decision
had not been too hasty, and that neither she nor
Mother could dream of undertaking such a journey
for the wedding. This saddened me, though I real-

ized that such a trip for the latter would be impossible.

The letter from Frank's mother was beautiful. In it she reminded me that we were both the babies of our families and, therefore, the hardest to part with, but she was glad that he had found someone to make a home for him and safeguard some of the habits of refinement that must be lacking in that rough country, and which he had missed.

The Black Hills Campaign

xii

OUTSIDE of our own youthful plans, Frank's letter dealt with the expedition. Up to the time of writing they had encountered no hostiles. Everyone was well, and the members of the scientific party proved to be a bunch of pretty good fellows. On one occasion Frank and Lieutenant Godfrey were detailed to accompany a few of these men to a point some distance away, where certain paleontologic deposits were expected to be found. The heat was intense, and the few small lakes they passed were as dry as Egyptian mummies.

That evening when they pitched camp the prairie felt as though it had been located on the top of a smoldering volcano, with not a breath of air stirring. The horses needed rest, food, and especially water, so the men drank sparingly, and no one dared waste even a few drops for shaving.

They slept fitfully and were up at dawn ready for further adventure. On they went, ploughing through the caked, arid earth which, when wet, was called "gumbo" and, strange to say, extremely fertile. This, the scientists declared, indicated volcanic matter somewhere and pushed on enthusiastically. But Old Sol kept up his relentless beating upon their skulls with as yet no scientific reward in evidence, and the whole party began to feel discouraged, when suddenly the jaded horses raised their heads, nostrils quivering, neighed, and sniffed the air, the dogs lifted their drooping tails and barked, and the men grabbed their long-distance field glasses and scanned the horizon. In the distance they saw something bluish, glimmering, and they shouted with joy. Water—water at last! It didn't need any urging to quicken their gait; the animals, with swollen tongues, saw to that, and in a short time they were almost upon the pond. Yet, as they approached it, something ominous crept over the men, for the color was not blue but green—grass green. Moreover, when they arrived at the edge a gruesome spectacle presented itself. The banks were covered with skeletons of animals and a few men, clad in tattered, faded garments, with some rusty tools scattered about. Prospectors, probably, caught in some strange web of destruction.

Abruptly the expedition halted, though the animals plunged in their frenzy to reach the pond. One dog did escape and, literally flinging himself into the water, drank long and thirstily, then crawled back onto the bank only to stiffen out in death. Poison! The pond was poisoned, but how, from what? They were too tired and disappointed to try to find out. Besides, it took every ounce of strength they possessed to hold the horses and prevent them from bolting straight into that green, sinister tarn. The little water that remained in the kegs was dealt out meagerly, and then arose the question whether to continue or return to camp.

It would take thirty-six hours to retrace their steps, and they still had an ample supply of rations, but dared they gamble on the possibility of finding drinkable water? Why not? The pond indicated the presence of moisture somewhere in that locality, and surely it couldn't all be bad, so they finally decided to take a chance and pushed on. About four o'clock in the afternoon they ran into a great surprise.

As they rounded a hill there loomed ahead of them a ranch—not a tumbled-down shack but a real ranch, where horses were grazing near by and cowpunchers lounged in the corrals. No one dreamed of striking a ranch so far west of Bismarck, and it seemed like a glimpse of paradise through their field glasses.

Meanwhile, the cowboys had spotted them and, flinging themselves across the bare backs of their horses, came loping out to meet them. At the head of them rode a tall, spare figure, who, with an Oxford accent, introduced himself as Nelson, owner of the ranch, and not only did he greet them cordially, but he brought fresh mounts and canteens of cool, sweet water. Whether English, Australian, or Canadian, this man certainly knew his West, and when they arrived at the low, rambling ranch house the cowhands led the enlisted men and their horses off for food and water while the rest of the expedition was housed in comfortable rooms. Best of all, at the back door of the ranch house spouted an artesian well. It seemed unbelievable, and when Chinese servants appeared bearing rubber bathtubs and more water, the men wondered if the intense heat had made them a bit balmy.

When they had shaved and bathed, Mr. Nelson invited them downstairs for refreshments.

"Gosh!" ejaculated Lieutenant Godfrey, "but I could do with a long drink of whiskey." But he didn't get it—not then. Instead, a Chinese boy rolled into the spacious living room a table bristling with a teapot and homemade biscuits.

The men's eyes bulged with astonishment. Then, suddenly, they were threatened with almost uncontrollable laughter, but they managed to swallow it with the tea. The scientists, however, accepted everything as a matter of course, apparently never questioning the incongruity of afternoon tea being served out on the empty plains and to a hard-boiled set of men at that. Notwithstanding, there was nothing effeminate about their host. He proved to be a hard rider, hard drinker, and splendid shot, but the conventional roots of his native land still clung. While finishing his last cup of tea he announced that he was giving a dinner party that evening, creating more stupefied surprise. Wonder arose as to where he was to procure his guests, but this he explained quickly.

"You see, when I came out here I was the first rancher in these parts to go in for cattle raising. Now the field is becoming cluttered."

"Cluttered?" echoed Frank blankly, because even this ranch was not on the maps.

"Yes," continued his host, "there are two more cattle ranches, twenty-five miles apart—my neighbors, so to speak—and they will by my guests to-night with, of course, yourselves."

Panic seized the members of the expedition, and one of the scientists spoke up diffidently, "But, Mr. Nelson, we are none of us prepared for a social gathering. We've no adequate clothing."

"No," Lieutenant Godfrey hastened to agree, glancing down at his own and Frank's shabby, stained, dust-ingrained uniforms.

"And," chimed in Frank, "we have sufficient rations for our expedition, so if we can have some water, we can pitch our camp out on the plains in an hour."

"Not at all—not at all," protested their host. "I rarely have company, and it's deucedly lonely out here all by myself with just a handful of cowhands and Chinese to talk to," and there was such a wistful ring of sincerity in his voice that the men consented to remain for the night.

About six-thirty the guests began to arrive, a motley crew of ranchmen, dressed as such, with their wives in buckskin chaps and wearing sombreros.

At sight of them the others felt better. If it was going to be that sort of party, why all right. The women chatted gaily with everyone, the men intermingling in a friendly manner. Suddenly there was a step on the stair, and once again officers and scientists stared with bulging eyes, for down came their host, in immaculate evening clothes, as though attending a London social function. Again our contingent was torn between consternation and laughter, but not so the ranch outfit. They knew him of old and paid no attention to his Piccadilly clothes. The women greeted him noisily, and he simply chortled with delight.

Here, happily, the Chinese appeared with whiskey and soda, which was gratefully received by all. The liquor, though bad, was the best obtainable, and no one cared. Their host sat back, adjusted his monocle, sipped his highball in great good humor, and beamed upon his guests. The man had intended no superiority, but the old England in his blood simply would not down, irrespective of time, conditions, or place.

Of course, the mysterious tarn was discussed. The ranchers, while acknowledging its poisonous existence, knew nothing of its cause, but some suggestions were made, one being a superabundance of copper. However, it proved of value in ridding that part of the country of hostiles, who considered it a curse laid upon the land by the Great Spirit.

The dinner was a great success, each one contributing his or her share to the conversation, but it was their host who carried off the palm for adventures, and as he talked our own men listened in silence, speculating upon the fate that had cast this cultured man so far afield of his natural haunts. However, the plains were rife with just such unsolved mysteries. At three o'clock in the morning the ranchers threw themselves astride their rested mounts and blithely set out again for their homes.

Next morning the expedition started out anew, accompanied part way by Nelson, who seemed loath to lose them. In parting they urged him to join them into the Black Hills, but, looking silently over the prairies, he shook his head. And so they left him, while they pondered many things.

A Garrison Wedding
xiii

MY LETTER was drawing to a close when Iwilla came hurrying in from the kitchen with a package.

"Lordy, Miss Katie," she apologized, "I plumb forgot to give you this."

I took one glance at it and whooped for joy. "It looks like my wedding dress," I called to Mollie, immersed in her own mail.

With trembling fingers we untied the precious parcel, and, sure enough, the soft, white, shiny material gleamed before us like a pan of rich, unskimmed milk.

"Oh!" I exclaimed, "oh!" Seizing it, I ran down the row to Mrs. Custer's quarters. Here I found her with Maggie, Annie Yates, and Charlotte Moylan, and eagerly, as though they were being married themselves, they plunged into my wedding plans. My mother had also sent me a pattern, over which Mrs. Custer cast an experienced eye.

The next day we started to make my gown, Mrs. Custer doing the cutting and fitting, I the straight sewing, and Mrs. Moylan and Mollie the fancy hemming and ruffling, the others taking a hand from time to time and lending suggestions. Of course, we had no machine, but with so many willing hands the work progressed rapidly, and the summer sped away on wings.

"Bear Butte," near the Black Hills, South Dakota.

Letters from our men we brought to the sewing bee, because there were always items of interest omitted by some and supplied by others, so we followed closely everything pertaining to the expedition. All conceded the adventure into the new wilderness to be one of surprise, pleasure, and much acquired knowledge. The wily Indian remained elusive, but there were plenty of them, as was evident by many hastily abandoned camps. Still the soldiers pressed into the heart of the Black Hills, where they were held spellbound by nature's sheer, awesome beauty, while a great variety of game made hunting a favorite pastime. The Belle Fourche yielded quantities of catfish which, though somewhat tasteless, made a change of diet at least. Bear Butte, the huge extinct volcano which faces Fort Meade today, was a thing of such stark, stupendous grandeur that it seemed almost like a mirage to the men accustomed to the stretches of desolate prairie, and the virgin soil surrounding this upheaval of countless ages ago was singularly fertile. Around the base of the mountain was discovered a quantity of exquisite pink marble, some of which in later years Lieutenant de Rudio sculptured into delicate vases and other works of art for his quarters at Fort Meade.

"What a location for a garrison!" exclaimed General Custer.

All sorts of minerals abounded in these hills, and pink and white quartz in chunks that one could kick out of the soil with one's boot. The extraordinary growth and abundance of wild flora were the scientists' dream of joy, and into ravines and canyons they would disappear for several days.

Water was plentiful, and tall, black-green pine trees emitted penetrating, refreshing aromas. The men, impelled by the novelty of it all, delved into petrified forests and crystal caves, where hundreds of coyotes slunk by day and yapped by night. When the expedition reached the farthest foothills of the mountains, they ran into what were later termed Bad Lands, because no vegetation would grow there. Here, in contrast to the luxurious Black Hills proper, they confronted a fantastic desert, composed of barren, volcanic matter, mounds of it, multicolored, and ranging from palest blues to deepest crimson. These natural deposits sprawled across the wilderness like colossal elephants, camels, and other creatures, switching at times into Oriental temples. If these things created a feeling of awe in the sober-minded in broad daylight, what might they do in the moonlight to anyone who had fallen from sobriety?

Not a blade of grass, not a tree stump was visible, but the place was alive with rattlers, which made good eating. Of course, the farther the detachment penetrated into the mountain fastnesses the rarer became the letters, as it took scouts, detailed to carry and bring back the mail, a longer time to reach the outposts of civilization.

Personally, I was far too busy getting ready for the great day to think of much else. My fluffy summer dresses needed refurbishing and laundering, and here my spirits drooped a little, because

"Rise," though a good cook, was not a fancy laundress. However, Mollie solved the problem, for she summoned to our aid the wife of Sergeant Nash, who was the superlaundress of the regiment. She was a tall, thin Mexican whom the sergeant had picked up on the border, and there was little her long, slim fingers couldn't handle. Swarthy of countenance, black-eyed, with a mass of thick black hair, she nevertheless preserved the Latin coquetry of always wearing a veil. "So bad theese vinds," she complained, "for a jung girl's complexion," which, though true, was surprising, inasmuch as she had passed her pristine youth. She used to wash exclusively for the soldiers, but when the women of the garrison discovered her artistry in laundering delicate materials, the enlisted men's washing knew her no more. Not only had she all she could do for the officers' families at Lincoln, but some indiscreet woman had whispered the secret to the officers' wives of the infantry post as well, which brought her an avalanche of work.

In fact, Sergeant Nash grew fat and lazy on Mexican tamales and boasted that, with the money his wife was making, he intended, when his enlistment expired, to purchase a ranch and join the army of pioneers. However, laundering was not her only talent. No party was complete without her culinary assistance, and few births occurred without her expert help. She was a careful midwife, no less an embryo trained nurse, and she handled those babies not only with efficiency but with marked tenderness as well.

"What a pity you have no children of your own, Mrs. Nash," Mollie was moved to remark one day.

"Ah, Senora," came the reply, her slender hand resting lightly on her flat chest, "it is not given to us all to be mothers," and she turned away with a sigh.

"Oh," cried Mollie contritely, "forgive me. I didn't mean to hurt you."

"Eet ees nozzing, Senora," murmured Mrs. Nash gently.

My wedding arrangements were about completed. My gown was finished, and Mollie was making orange blossoms from little tufts of satin, using tiny threads of yellow embroidery silk for the centers. The garrison was agog with excitement, for some of the women from Rice were coming to meet their husbands returning from the campaign and were bringing their full-dress uniforms for the wedding. Mrs. Benteen, of course, would be our guest, while the others found welcome quarters elsewhere in the post. She had obligingly brought Frank's outfit with the colonel's.

The campaigners pulled into camp at dawn on August 30. Already the crispness of autumn was reaching out chill fingers during the night and early morning hours. None of the women rode out to meet them, because everyone was helping Mollie and me in our last-minute details of the wedding. The day before, soldiers had swarmed all over the house downstairs, had hung a cotton wedding bell in the window of the living room, and had stretched white canvas over the floors of the parlor and dining room, while Mrs. Nash had darted up and down ladders, stringing bright-colored cheesecloth draperies here and there. Iwilla kept coming in from the kitchen, complaining to Mollie, "Miss McIntosh, dat onery army punch ain't got de right punch in it yet." The beverage referred to had a base of strong tea with whiskey and citric acid.

About noon the men began to trickle into the garrison. They were the most disreputable-looking lot I ever saw. Many wore beards. Their faces were burned to dull reds and browns, and their campaign hats and flannel shirts were utterly ruined with alkali dust.

Frank and Donald, looking more like Indians than white men, swung from their saddles and came bounding up the steps. The first thing they asked for was plenty of water, inside and out, because once they had left the Black Hills the country had gone bone dry, as there had been practically no rainfall for weeks. Mollie and Donald greeted each other as though the separation had covered two years instead of two months, and Frank and I—well, I guess I must have swallowed a pound or two of dust and horse's hair as well, gladly. We had a million things to say and no time in which to say them. Frank showed me a check from the bachelors as a wedding gift to us. The women had made me presents of pretty handmade underwear; faithful Iwilla had contributed two small towels of unbleached linen, which she had embroidered with blue cornflowers. Mrs. Custer ran over with a dainty blue garter for the "something new and blue" to complete my wedding costume. Mollie loaned me our mother's brooch of moonstones surrounded by pearls and tiny diamonds, all of which made me very happy.

There was only one fly in the ointment. Frank's flowers, ordered weeks ago from St. Paul, arrived at the eleventh hour so frosted from the sudden drop in temperature that they were beyond resuscitation. They were a kind of aster, as roses simply did not exist out there in those days, and what to do about a bouquet became the burning question. Of course, we might dig up a prayerbook, but it would take time to cover it with white satin.

Maggie Calhoun came to the rescue. She suddenly appeared with a box containing long stalks of soapweed she had hastily gathered on the plain. This peculiar plant (the root of which was often used for soap because of its lather) consisted of thick, fibrous stalks that ranged in length from one to perhaps three feet. It bore huge, white, scentless blossoms, bell-like in shape and resembling a mammoth lily of the valley. Had they been roses or white orchids we could not have fallen upon them with more gratitude. Straightway we wound the stalks with strips of white satin, and then laid the whole sheath lengthwise on my arm. Stretch your imagination as you may, you could not visualize anything prettier.

And now Mollie was hurrying me upstairs to be dressed. Charlotte Moylan and Maggie followed, saying, "You get dressed yourself, Mrs. McIntosh. We'll help Katie."

I could hear the clank of sabers hitting against the bannisters as the young officers sprang up the stairs two at a time and clattered into the back room where Frank was struggling into his regalia. I heard merry laughter and the voice of Captain Moylan bawling, "Clear out—for Christ's sake! How can he dress, you——"

I used to marvel at first at these vitriolic explosions, but soon sensed that they were merely forms of airy bombast to which no one paid the slightest attention. Lieutenant Mathey, affectionately called "Bible Thumper," performed this art with such skill and originality that he was unanimously voted the star blasphemy-hurler of the regiment. He blamed it on his family; they had forced him to study for the priesthood in France, which resulted in his being driven into agnosticism and finally going by the steerage to America, where he joined our army.

Following Captain Moylan's protests came the retreating feet and the sound of sabers again, as they banged on the steps. Yes, they were all there, those happy boys. Few were married, and all care-free; they faced life with untroubled minds, without one presentiment of what fate had in store for them not so many months away.

I also heard the opening and shutting of doors —guests arriving; the aroma of venison and prairie chicken and ham assailed one's nostrils, while joyous excitement pervaded the entire house.

Dressed at last, I needed no artificial coloring, for my cheeks were ablaze with happy nervousness.

Mollie, looking very handsome, came into my room with the veil, and, as she adjusted it, I saw her eyes were misty. I sensed her realization that she was taking the place of our lady-mother, but she covered her emotion by warning briskly, "For goodness' sake, don't fall over your train or tear your veil. And when I start the wedding march don't lag, but come on downstairs." She then left us abruptly.

A few minutes later I heard the strains of the wedding march. Maggie Calhoun handed me my unique bouquet, then adjusted my train. On very trembling legs I wobbled downstairs. And what a sight met my eyes! The room and hall were packed with gaily gowned women, while officers were re-splendent in their full-dress uniforms. At the foot of the stairs Donald gave me his arm, and I walked the length of the living room toward the wedding bell, where the chaplain awaited us. On the right was my beloved, clean-shaved and as handsome as a god, while beside him was Captain Moylan, his best man. Then Frank took my hand, and we stood beneath the bell as Donald stepped a little away from me. Every time I glanced at him his smile and kind eyes braced me for the plunge. When he gave me away, somehow his deep-toned, positive voice assured me that all was well.

As soon as the last words were spoken, General Custer and Captain Moylan, each on one side of us, crossed sabers over our heads, and instantly every officer sprang to the same position while we passed beneath an arch of metal into the dining room. At the end of the line, a tassel from handsome Lieutenant Van Riley's uniform caught for a second in my hair, whereupon the wearer called out gaily, "See, Gibby, fate protests that she should have married me."

"Not at all," denied Benny Hodgson vigorously. "I met her first."

"What of it?" contended Lieutenant Cook, regimental adjutant. "Didn't I stage a full-dress parade in her honor?"

"Yes, you did," sneered Jimmy Porter. "Too bad she had to share it with the visiting inspector." At this everyone guffawed loudly.

Captain Tom Custer nipped a piece of icing off the uncut cake.

"Well, who taught her to ride, I'd like to know?" he asked, munching.

"Hey, hey!" protested the General. "I claim part of the credit for both her riding and shooting, but unfortunately I'm not a Turk."

And so the merriment and ragging went on, while I cut the cake with my husband's saber. Everyone had a wonderful time.

Colonel and Mrs. Tilford, Colonel and Mrs. Merrill, and Major Reno and his wife congregated in one corner of the crowded room, the Custers with their coterie in another, while Mollie and Donald were ubiquitous, looking after the interests of their guests. And how many there were—hall, living room, dining room, even the kitchen packed.

Some had come from a distance, like Lieutenant Winfield Edgerly (afterwards a general), who had obtained leave of absence from Fort Totten, Dakota, just to "see Gibby safely through the ordeal," he laughingly explained. And then dear Old Gothic, who got out of a sickbed—for his wound was troubling him again—to hobble over and wish us joy. And, of course, Lieutenant Wallace, and Lieutenant and Mrs. Harrington, and Nave and Weston and Nolan and Captains French, Keogh, and the Calhouns; in fact, most of the officers of the regiment were present and some from the infantry post as well.

When it came to drinking the health of the bride and groom every eye glanced surreptitiously at General Custer, wondering what he would do. As the toast was proposed and given, he nodded smilingly, lifted the punch to his lips, wet them slightly, then replaced his glass, practically untouched. However, considering that he was a total abstainer, Frank and I felt that he had paid us a particular honor in swallowing even a few drops.

Lieutenant de Rudio had just bought a new fulldress uniform, the trimmings of which were very expensive, especially the gold braid, cords, tassels, and belt. The gayness of it attracted the attention of a small boy who was usually frescoed from head to foot with molasses; hence, when the glittering gold lured him as the lieutenant sat down beside him, his sticky little fingers just naturally strayed to the ornaments until, as the officer explained in broken English, "When he put hees hand on my epaulets again, I reach up and cover eet wiz my own, and I say, 'Nice leetle boy, nice leetle boy,' and I *craunch* eet." And thus tactfully terminated the sugary experiment.

Southern Interlude

xiv

NEXT DAY the Rice detachment left early, and, as I waved to my husband, I gloried in the fact that now I was really one with the other army women, and our joys and sorrows would be mutual.

From now on the garrison surged with excitement. The homes of the officers detailed for Southern duty were dismantled and the contents stored; and even a snowstorm on the tenth of September couldn't dampen our spirits, for soon we would be basking in the warm, semitropical sunshine.

On the twenty-eighth the Rice contingent rejoined the Lincoln detachment, this time headed for the Department of the Gulf. Such a cavalcade came with the troops from Rice that ambulances of all kinds were pressed into service to bring the wives and children of those destined for the next day's trip. It took some good-natured doubling-up to accommodate the temporary visitors, but no one minded. Mrs. Benteen and a small child bunked in Mollie's room, and Mrs. de Rudio and two urchins in mine, one of whom walked up and down my back all night. The men camped out on carpenter's-horse tables all over the house.

The following day we entrained for the South, and the wistful good-bys and good wishes of our friends left us momentarily a bit homesick.

And what a trip that was! It might have been described as a six-day picnic, and though we passed over practically the same route that I took four months earlier it proved quite different, owing to the presence of the United States Army. I never realized before what a potent influence that uniform wielded in those troublous times.

No more food grabbing—that was done for us. No more bandit scares. Before we reached the Middle West the snow had vanished and the weather began to grow warmer as piece by piece we shed our heavy clothing until, when we reached New Orleans, the women and children were parad ing in full summer attire. The journey had been practically perfect, barring the bloody noses and knocked-out teeth of the children swinging in the aisles and a certain amount of physical discomfort engendered through the gluttonous indulgence of tropical fruits, to which our youngsters were un-accustomed. Real ice cream was the great luxury, eaten at all hours of the day or night by grown-ups as well. Mollie was infantile in her absorption, and it had to be as hard as brick to suit her. On one occasion some well-meaning young officer thought he was bringing her a rare treat in the flavor he had selected. And here cropped up an-other of her idiosyncrasies. I do not know to this day the cause of her violent antipathy to chocolate. Perhaps her antagonism to the color of brown had something to do with it, but, when the young fellow smilingly brought her a plate of chocolate ice cream, she took one look at it, then raged, and was about to throw it out of the window, when little Freddy Benteen relieved her of it. He and small Roma de Rudio finished it.

New Orleans presented a marvelous sight to our prairie-trained eyes. Instead of yellow, parched grasses, the "banquets" of the quaint old city flaunted their gay green, and there were flowers, flowers, everywhere. I stared at the quantities of heavily scented roses, ridiculously cheap in price, comparing them to my bridal bouquet of just a few weeks ago. I tried to hypnotize myself into the belief that mine was prettier; at least it was more original.

As Jackson Barracks was not quite ready to receive us, a number of us went to boardinghouses. Mollie and Donald were detailed to Shreveport, so here we reluctantly parted.

Unfortunately, we saw little of our men. They were called out all through the South to quell disturbances, leaving us pretty much alone.

However, we literally basked in this mellow climate which induced a surprising laziness, gave us good food, and nothing to do but enjoy band concerts, theaters, and long drives into the country. Speaking of these drives, Mrs. de Rudio and I had a peculiar experience during one of them. The day was intensely warm, and, passing a farmhouse, we suddenly decided that we just had to have a glass of cold milk. So we instructed our negro driver to stop. A courteous Creole woman who spoke little English received us with quaint formality and ushered us into the house. Then she excused herself, and we sat down in the best room, which was darkened by drawn blinds to keep out the heat. We had been there only a moment or two when I sensed something strange about the place. My vision began to clear, and both Mrs. de Rudio and I sprang to our feet. Moving through the dimness we discerned a child about a year old—but such a child! It was wriggling forward on its belly. Its little head was triangular in shape, pendent from a long neck that undulated as it crawled. Two small beady eyes flickered from under a low brow, and between its parted lips a tongue slid quickly from side to side in the manner of a snake. The appearance of this peculiar baby was so upsetting that we were about to flee from the room when the woman returned with milk and cookies. We swallowed the refreshments, still standing, paid for them, and, making some excuse for our abrupt flight, got into our carriage and drove away.

The atmosphere of the boardinghouse was homey. Besides several army families temporarily installed there, we met a Monsieur and Madame de Vergnette, a charming young French couple just recently married. They proved to be a distinct addition to our social group, for they were both musical, played cards, and joined in all the fun. We became quite attached to them.

November brought chill and penetrating rains. Unhealthy, dank odors escaped from some of the narrow streets, especially in those parts of the old French Quarter we liked to visit. Then hospital ambulances began to appear, becoming more numerous. Great placards bearing the dread word, "QUARANTINE," defaced the fronts of some houses, while with bated breath people whispered, "small-pox," and wholesale vaccination was imposed.

Our men were away so much that, personally, they had little to fear from city contagion. But we were anxious, especially the mothers with children. Our landlady, however, assured us that there wasn't the slightest danger. So that day at luncheon, when Monsieur de Vergnette appeared with a few pimples on his forehead, we paid no attention to it. But at dinner his face looked startlingly red, and an unmistakable rash was visible.

The young couple failed to join us later in the drawing room as was their custom. The rest of us naturally grouped together and discussed what was to be done, but we decided to wait until morning for further developments.

The de Vergnettes were not at breakfast, and a chilled silence fell upon us. At ten o'clock a hospital ambulance drew up at our door, and a young intern asked the location of the de Vergnettes' room, which was found to be at the head of the stairs. Solemnly the doctor and his men tramped up and knocked at their door. There came the voice of the frightened little bride, "Who is it?"

"Dr. Monceau from the City Hospital," he said, and then added, "Open the door." But the girl-wife called back that there must be some mistake, because no one was ill there. The doctor nevertheless kept insisting that he be admitted.

"Otherwise I shall break down the door," he finished sharply. That brought results. I was coming along the hall myself at the time, and as the portal swung open I caught a glimpse of the poor thing. Her black hair was tumbling down her back, accentuating the pallor of her usually pale face. Great circles under her eyes told tales of a sleepless night.

She stood before the figure of her husband on the bed, trying with her puny strength to keep them away from him, screaming and clawing at the men's faces when they started to move him. When finally they carried him out on a stretcher, she threw herself on the floor and gave way to a torrent of tears. During this scene my lurking presence was unnoticed, but I was so unstrung over her agony that I think I would have gone to her had not levelheaded Mrs. de Rudio, who had also been upstairs, taken hold of me and given me a good shake.

"Are you crazy to go into that room?" she demanded sternly.

And that was the last pitiful chapter of the newlyweds, because he never returned. After it was all over, the poor little bride disappeared as completely as though the ground had opened and snatched her and her broken heart to its bosom. Of course, we too were now quarantined. How to reach our men was the question. No person or thing could leave that house, and while the postman would gingerly deposit our mail on the doorstep, he could take none from us.

As the place had to be fumigated, Madame Bridier, the landlady, lodged us in an empty, adjoining house, entered by way of her back yard. Cots and necessities were installed, and I began to wonder if my life was to become a permanent existence of camping. Here the Frenchwoman would funnel her grocery orders through a door crack to a scared colored boy, who stood champing like a restless pony at the end of the yard. Later he would return, drop a filled basket at the back door, and Mercury's wings were no swifter than his scampering, bare, black feet.

So we were literally prisoners during the city's war against the plague. When we demanded that our husbands and relatives be notified, Madame merely shrugged her shoulders, saying in broken English that the health authorities would attend to the matter, but personally she would take no chances of jeopardizing her boardinghouse permit by allowing any thing or person to enter or leave her premises. However, Mrs. de Rudio's little Creole nurse, as slim as a knife blade, evolved a plan. At night after dinner, while old Madame dozed in her chair, Babbette would slip through a narrow window, which we had pried open, and mail our letters. Of course, our safety was an immense relief to our men and families, for by now the city was in the throes of the epidemic. With brooding eyes we would gaze out of our bare windows at the ever-increasing number of ambulances tearing through the street. As there were insufficient transportation facilities, the Black Maria's had to be added, and these vehicles were passing, passing, all day and all night.

Meanwhile, the soldiers had returned to the barracks and were anxiously awaiting our freedom. Finally, a few days before Christmas, the quarantine was lifted, and never in my life was I so glad to see the old army ambulance standing at our door, ready to take us to the reservation.

I found my husband looking thin and tired from lack of sleep and being torn by anxiety over the increasing riots and my safety. Of course, the epidemic was now eliminated, "But," he said, "this duty is worse than Indian fighting because it is hard to prevent bloodshed among our own people."

However, we were happy just to be together, and I looked upon him as my very best Christmas present.

But the respite was brief, for the troops were soon called out again. Disturbances had broken out in Alabama, and heaven only knew when the soldiers would return. This last was more than I could bear, and I displayed no Spartan qualities. I just bawled; of course, I was very young, very much in love, and had not been born in the army. Frank was distressed by my tempest of tears and suggested a visit to my lady-mother, but I shook my head vehemently. I would be too far away from him, if he returned unexpectedly. Then would I go to Mollie? Again I protested and succeeded in making us both supremely miserable. Notwithstanding, the United States Government didn't wait for my emotions to simmer down, and, swallowing a sob, I watched him line up with his troop, his mount plunging with excitement, and the detachment get under way. I went home with understanding Mrs. Benteen, who had been married long enough to control her feelings.

She surprised me at lunch with a creole preparation of shrimps of which I was fond, but this wasn't the only bit of thoughtfulness that awaited me. As we were sitting down at the table, the swinging door shoved open, and who should stand upon the threshold but Mollie. It seemed that Donald, too, had been called out on duty, and Frank had urged her to come to Jackson Barracks and keep me company.

She was like a whiff of northern air to us all, and her visit did us lots of good. She was planning things to do every minute. She knew every card game under the sun, wielded a croquet mallet like a professional, played five musical instruments, and could tell a story better than anyone I ever heard.

The circus was in town, so of course we took it in. It was held in a huge tent on the outskirts of the city. We set forth for a gala day with an infantry colonel and his wife. The latter was ethereal-looking and had cultivated the habit of fainting at the slightest provocation. During this period *Children of the Abbey* was being widely read, which put the stamp of refinement upon delicate women. Fainting became the latest craze, and Mrs. ―――― had the art down to a science. Moreover, she learned it was a potent medium to attract men's attentions, bringing out their chivalrous and protective qualities admirably. One colonel's wife used to boast that she was so frail and helpless that she couldn't hem a pocket handkerchief. Unfortunately, Mollie and I were plebeianly healthy, and praying for sickly refinement did us no good whatever.

Well, we started for the circus in high feather. The tent was crowded, and we sat gingerly upon none too stable benches, which creaked uneasily at any sudden move. The show got under way, and while the animals and circus people did their stunts we imbibed the usual quantities of pink lemonade and munched on indigestible peanuts.

In the middle of the performance an elephant in the ring suddenly began to trumpet and look around. Others of the jungle fraternity, both inside and outside of the tent, immediately took up the refrain. The noise became louder and louder, and the lions and laughing hyenas mingled in violent discord. People began to move uneasily on their precarious perches and glance furtively about, but the din and confusion continued with unabating intensity.

A man sitting just behind Mollie leaned over and spoke to his companion, whereupon she rose instantly, nearly upsetting me. Mollie whispered, "He says a lion has got loose. Tell Colonel ———, and we will all leave quietly."

But somehow that dread information seemed to have permeated the whole tent, for the stampede began. Pandemonium reigned, drowning the voices of the circus attendants. Screaming children were dragged out by frightened parents; seats collapsed as frenzied people fought and trampled on each other in their mad rush for the exits, scattering all kinds of apparel: parasols, coats, bags, and slippers.

Meanwhile, our party had become separated, and I was borne along with the crowd. Something hard slipped under my feet—a set of false teeth mixed up with a few broken fans! Finally, I was projected like a bullet out of the tent and landed on the spongy sod where I rolled out of the way of countless feet.

The mob began to break up, darting off in all directions. Suddenly I heard Mollie's voice at my bruised elbow asking about the Colonel and Mrs. ————. Apparently she was not concerned regarding my possible injuries.

I shook my head, indicating my ignorance of their whereabouts, and got up rubbing my hip. Then, unexpectedly, Colonel ———— popped into sight, hatless, an epaulet gone, and every button ripped off his uniform blouse.

"Have you seen Mrs. ————?" he demanded in an agonized voice.

"No!" we both screamed above the din, shaking our heads vaguely.

Just then an attendant appeared, carrying what seemed to be a large bundle of rags. There was a familiar look about those rags—the cerulean blue silk, a shred of what used to be a real lace flounce. Instantly the colonel was beside the man, and, lifting the inert form from the sturdy arm, it proved to be Mrs. ———, fainting as usual.

The attendant explained. "I seen her lying un-conscious-like against an elephant, and the giraffe in the next stall was lickin' the spots offen her veil, so I figured she needed a little air." Mollie fanned her with the half of a fan she still clutched, while the colonel hurried away for water.

At this moment a colored boy was passing with a pail, and I hailed him. "Hey, boy," I inquired, "where's the loose lion that caused the stampede?"

"Lion, ma'am?" he repeated. "There ain't no loose lion— the animals always cuts up like that when it gets to feedin' time."

That visit to the circus provided conversation for months; in fact, it was one of Mollie's pet stories up to the day of her death.

The rest of the winter passed uneventfully, our only excitement being the going and coming of the troops.

The climate was divine, and fruits abundant and cheap, but we began to feel the lassitude and en-ervation so prevalent in semitropical countries. So it was almost with relief that we received orders calling us West again. Of course, it wrenched our hearts to leave our new friends stationed at the barracks, but that is one of the penalties ex-acted by the army. You may be stationed with these same people again, or you may never meet them again this side of heaven.

It had been my husband's intention to apply for a week's leave of absence, which would give us time to visit my lady-mother and take in Philadelphia as well, but it couldn't be managed. He wanted me to precede him and spend a few days with my family. But nothing could induce me to leave him, so we started to pull up stakes and join the regiment in Dakota again.

All the luggage had to leave with us on the train or be left behind; hence things were literally hurled into army chests. All the children's clothing had been stowed away in one huge chest with a spring lock, but in the extreme haste the keys had been left inside. The lid had gone down with a bang, the force pushing arms and legs of garments over the sides.

Consternation prevailed, there being no time to do anything, and the chest could not go as military baggage in that condition. So a soldier with a hatchet trimmed off the offending articles like piecrust, and the children had to wear them that way when they reached their destination.

The children of the Indian scouts, watching ours at play, thought these garments a new fashion, so off came an arm and leg of each little buckskin suit. Thus a new mode was born.

Back to Dakota

xv

WE LEFT Louisiana on May 5 and arrived at Yankton, Dakota, on May 11, where we were instructed to await A and E troops en route north.

This dashing back and forth across the continent had ceased to be a novelty to me. The picturesqueness of the plains, the slowly moving, slowly vanishing oxcarts, the elusive Indian villages that became more and more frequent as we journeyed West—all these were the same story.

We had resumed wearing our heavy clothing, for winter out there retreated leisurely. The only harbinger of spring was the enterprising crocus which thrust its saucy, purple head from time to time through the snow, patches of which still lingered.

Yankton, termed by courtesy a city, consisted of a few houses built of cottonwood or fresh pine, some rutted dirt roads, and a frame hostelry called a hotel. This establishment was little more than a glorified barn, the floor of the living room being strewn with sawdust upon which perched a quantity of cuspidors. The rooms lacked paint or paper, and the walls were full of knotholes. Some of the accommodations had threadbare strips of narrow carpet sprawled beside springless, wooden beds, but for the most part there was nothing to step on but bare boards. The furniture consisted of little more than camping outfits.

We arrived late at night and were fortunate to find a vacant room. As we entered in the dark, the sound of raucous voices halted us for a moment, and ribald laughter boomed through slack, liquor-logged lips. Poker chips clicked and changed hands in the next room, the winners howling with glee, the losers cursing their luck.

I paused on the threshold of our room, wide-eyed and speechless, for my husband had slipped his hand quickly over my mouth.

"No noise," he whispered. "They must not know this room is occupied." And I realized what he meant. They must not know that a *woman* was there. Silently we slipped off our boots and shoes in the darkness, and, fully dressed, we stole to the hard bed, where we stretched our weary bodies, but not to sleep. That was impossible, for, with our neighbors bawling their songs midst the clatter of poker chips and the ringing sound of tin cups as they drank and drank, bedlam was certainly let loose. Finally my husband rose quietly and peered through a knothole, where he remained for quite a few minutes. Then he came toward me, and unconsciously I felt that his body had become taut with suppressed excitement.

"Listen," he whispered grimly. "I'm going into that room."

"No, no!" I answered in agony. "Those brutes will kill you!"

"I've got to go," he reiterated. "But here's an

extra revolver. Keep it near you and remain here. If anyone attempts to molest you, fire."

He thrust the weapon into my trembling hands, slipped noiselessly into his boots, and, cat-like, stole out of the room. For a moment I could hear my heart beat as I strained my ears to listen for his boots as they slid along the corridor. I flew to the knothole in stocking feet just as he knocked on the door.

"Open this door!" commanded Frank.

Taut silence followed for a couple of seconds, then, "Who is it?" snapped a voice that somehow stirred me. Chairs grated sharply against the floor as they were pushed back.

I saw a long, crude wooden table, lighted by tallow candles and covered with cards, chips, and piles of gold. Involuntarily I gasped, for never had I seen so much wealth. Gathered about this Croesus board were seated rough, weather-beaten men, big, rangy, and low-browed, dressed in plaid flannel shirts open at the neck, and wearing worn buckskin trousers stuffed into high boots. Each one clutched a revolver in his red, rawboned hand, while another one was stuck in his belt. A row of uncorked whiskey bottles stood on the table.

Still the silence held until Frank's voice replied.

"Another gambler."

There was a pause, then the first man rasped, "How much you got?"

"Plenty."

Here came another pause, during which I died a thousand deaths; my feet were rooted to the floor, my hand that held the revolver, numb. What would happen now? The man nearest the door opened it cautiously and peered out. Instantly my husband thrust his boot inside the panel and, shoving it violently with his shoulder, sprang into the room, his revolver trained—on one man. He faced him with steely determination.

At sight of an officer the gamblers fell back, but the face of the man Frank was covering turned white; then, instinctively, his hand went to his forehead in a salute. Meanwhile, Frank had advanced slowly toward him. Still the other hung back.

"You're wanted, Thompson, by the United States Government for robbing your company funds and deserting from the Seventh Cavalry," rapped out the lieutenant, his voice as cold as the muzzle of his gun. By this time he had reached the culprit, who seemed too dazed to act. Frank snatched his revolver from under his eyes and jerked his head, indicating the prisoner to precede him out of the room. My knees began to shake. What would happen to my man now? Would they shoot him in the back, this slender, boyish officer? And then a spring in me must have been released, for the blood surged into my right arm again and stiffened it. Slowly I raised my gun toward that knothole. Whoever touched him, I vowed grimly, would pay with his own life.

But here Frank broke the tension himself. With his gun nudging the ribs of Thompson, he turned to the others with his old flashing smile. "Sorry

not to be able to join you tonight, boys, but—er—
ask me again sometime."

I held my breath at his impudence. What now?
Still no man moved. Why? Was it a grudging
respect for the uniform, or the youngster who wore
it, or both? At any rate, they permitted captor
and captive to leave the room unharmed, and with
relief my arm dropped to my side.

Here the leader, just out of range of my vision,
spoke authoritatively. Again my memory strained
at its leash, for that voice was vaguely familiar.

"All for tonight, boys. Let's go," he ordered
crisply, and suddenly they seemed to become sober,
all but one hulking giant who weighed over two
hundred pounds and who remained staggeringly
drunk. The others swept gold and cards into heavy
bags, blew out the candles, and trickled into the
hall. I heard my husband pass the locked door of
our room with the deserter, and one by one the
gamblers straggled by. Suddenly the drunken
giant lost his balance and lunged against the thin,
cottonwood panel of my door, splitting it with his
weight as neatly as though it had been cleaved
with an axe, and he plunged straight into my room.
The moment was tense with mutual surprise, then,
pulling himself together, he flashed an evil smile,
revealing his tobacco-stained teeth.

"A woman, by God!" he boomed. "A woman
with golden hair!" And in an instant he had seized
my wrist, and, shaking the revolver out of my
wobbling hand, he picked me up in his gorilla arms
as easily as though I had been a baby. I tried to

scream, but words stuck in my throat, and my puny fists that beat upon him were like so many flies buzzing on his face. Horror numbed me as I felt my strength ebbing, and I began to flounder mentally when there came a quick, incisive voice.

"Put that woman down!"

The giant hesitated.

"Put her down, I say!" it snapped in a higher key, and I felt myself slipping to the floor. The broken door let in a flood of light from the kerosene lamp in the hall, and as I looked up I gasped. Beside me, cool and dapper-looking, stood my old friend and fellow playmate, Doc Wilson. So, *his* was the voice vaguely familiar. Recognition was mutual, but neither of us gave sign. We measured each other in silence. The pretty speech I had prepared for him a year ago went completely away as I stammered, "Thank you," adding, with a little rush of breath, "And God bless you, Robin Hood."

At that, his eyes bored into mine for a moment, then, with a wave of his hand that was reminiscent of our last encounter, he stepped into the narrow hall and vanished. Several moments elapsed before my common sense returned. "What have I done?" I asked myself frantically, the finger of accusation pointed at me. "You have allowed an outlaw to escape—that pile of gold in the next room was stolen; besides, a reward of five thousand dollars had been put upon his head—and army officers are poor."

Instinctively I ran toward the door—if only I could stop him before it was too late—before——.

And then, strangely enough, I realized that I had no desire to stop him. Twice this man had done me a great service. Besides, I thought, trying to whitewash my conscience, he was bound to be caught someday. So, when Frank and the sheriff had duly locked up the deserter, and the former returned, I made light of the giant losing his balance and paying me an unexpected visit.

I even did some clever mimicking, and it wasn't until months later that I told him the truth, to which he had remarked, after a pause, "I'm glad you didn't tell me."

The next week or two was taken up welcoming the troops back from the South. Then the men left Yankton with troops A and E for Fort Randall.

As my husband was likely to be campaigning nearly all summer, it was decided that I would pass part of it with the Yateses at Lincoln before joining him at Fort Rice.

Mollie and Donald were to remain in the South. At first I missed them terribly. Looking back upon those few weeks of the summer that preceded the Custer Massacre, when everyone was so happy and hopeful that these Indian disturbances would soon cease, I am glad that I did remain with those women for a time, because when next I saw them tragedy had struck at them, streaking their still young heads with silver.

Still in camp opposite Fort Randall, near the town of White Swan, were troops A, E, and H. They were constantly making excursions into the surrounding country, for time and time again they

were ordered to the Ponca Indian Agency to cool
the blood of refractory young braves and other
Indians who were eternally hectoring the citizens
by stealing their livestock and supplies. On these
occasions the soldiers usually took as prisoners a
number of these troublemakers and their squaws.
One sizzling hot day, while these lawbreakers were
being brought into camp, my husband saw a very
young squaw drop out of line and steal behind a
bush. A bit curious, he waited a short distance
away to see what she was up to. Imagine his surprise to see her emerge holding in her arms a
brand-new papoose. Having caught up with the
others, she plodded through the scorching dust as
though nothing had happened. The perspiration,
though, was pouring down her face, and the new-
born brave was wailing.

The sight of these forlorn creatures brought
back recollections of that other prairie birth at
which Frank had been present. No matter what
race, creed, or color, the agony of childbearing is
the same all over the world. A great pity welled
in Frank's heart for the young savage mother and
her baby, so he stopped one of the government
wagons and made her get in it, seeing to it that
they both were given plenty of water. The woman
drank long and forced some down the throat of the
wee one, but she said nothing. Her man, trudging
along behind the wagon, looked on in sullen silence.

The Indians, however, were not the only ones
to give the troops trouble. Certain bands of law-
less miners were determined to enter the Black

Hills against military orders. From July 15 until August 26, when they rounded up and brought into camp forty-four miners as prisoners, the soldiers were scouting all over the country, camping back and forth on the Cheyenne River, Cannon Ball Creek, and French Creek. Finally things settled down, and they left Fort Randall on September 20, arriving at Rice, for winter quarters, October 7.

Meanwhile, I was comparatively comfortable at Lincoln, and though I did feel a bit forlorn seeing others occupy Mollie's old quarters, everyone was so wholeheartedly glad to have me with them, and the regimental band was such a joy, that I made myself happy; besides, I was getting ready for my first army home. Mollie had loaned me her piano for the winter, as they hardly expected to return before spring. Maggie Calhoun was staying with the Custers for a while, as Lieutenant Calhoun was away with the rest of the troops, and we did have good times together.

Annie Yates was a perfect hostess, because she wasn't rushing you into some activity every moment. Although she was full of fun and sympathetic understanding, you felt free to go and come and do what you pleased in her house, as if it were your own home. We spent a lot of time at the Custers, which seemed to be the mecca for everyone. Then, too, I had the opportunity of really getting to know others in the regiment.

Colonel and Mrs. Tilford were always entertaining, and we had picnics galore. Then there were Colonel and Mrs. Merrill, General and Mrs. Sturgis—whose handsome son, Jack, had just graduated from West Point and was to be stationed with us at Rice—and many more.

The men, of course, were busy with their routine work. General Custer and some of his staff would make trips for days at a time. The General loved hunting and used to wear for that purpose a buckskin suit with cap to match. When he started off with thirty or forty dogs all set for the chase, he would be as happy as a small boy.

I divided my time among the Yateses, Charlotte Moylan, and the Custers. The General, by the way, taught me cribbage.

So things jogged along uneventfully, until one day the garrison received a shock. Mrs. Nash suddenly died. The cause of her death was somewhat vague, but today the medical profession would probably diagnose it as appendicitis. Anyway, the regimental laundress, midwife, and cook was no more. She was a great loss, and at first there was felt consternation, a feeling which soon gave way to a growing indignation. People demanded what right she had to make a glutton of herself on unripe corn, when so many were dependent upon her skillful, Latin fingers for delicate laundering. Besides, the stork was threatening to alight at any moment upon several chimneys. It wasn't fair, they all contended.

But the worst was yet to come. Mrs. Nash proved not to have been Mrs. Nash at all. Neither had she been an Aztec princess in disguise, nor a nun who had fled from religious persecution. She

turned out to have been someone much more pro-
saic—in short, she had been a man! At this discovery, indignation mounted to hysteria, and the
news spread quickly from Lincoln to the infantry
post. Her untimely passing made front-page news
for the one-sheet weekly paper, and the usual murder cases and stories of Indian cutups were pushed
back among the ads.

Rumors about Mrs. Nash filtered through the
reservation as far as Bismarck, where her Mexican
tamales were conceded to be of the best. And this
is what was whispered, though Sergeant Nash
neither affirmed nor denied anything.

It seemed that some years before, a certain po-
litical fugitive escaped across the Mexican border
and disappeared. Sergeant Nash happened to be
stationed in that section at the time, and it was
claimed that, simultaneously with the vanishing
fugitive, a swarthy man disguised as a woman approached the sergeant, whom he had met at sundry
gambling joints along the border. He bribed the
soldier to go through a marriage ceremony with
him (or her), thus giving the culprit the protection of the American flag. Aside from the cupidity
aroused in the sergeant, there were certain advantages to be gained by such a move. Married
soldiers enjoyed more freedom than the untrammeled enlisted men. They were given individual
quarters and did not have to eat in barracks; moreover, their wives were permitted to work as do-
mestics on the reservation, thereby swelling the
family exchequer. A last consideration was the

sergeant's weakness for Mexican cooking. So, goaded by greed and his appetite, he introduced his veiled bride to the regiment. Indoors she discarded the veil, worn in the light both summer and winter, and if one, from time to time, noticed a bit of down on her lips, one reflected that Latin women as they grow older are prone to develop hair on their faces and let it pass at that. What subsequently became of Sergeant Nash? My impression is that he took up ranching, but that I cannot vouch for.

Lieutenant Nolan, regimental quartermaster for the time being, promised to see about the shipment of Mollie's piano to Fort Rice, whenever I wanted it. The quartermaster sergeant respectfully suggested that it be sent fairly soon, owing to the uncertainty of the weather, but I vetoed the idea, as I wanted to settle my house first and decided upon the middle of September, with the result that the boat which transported it froze solidly in the ice somewhere between the two garrisons, where it remained until spring. Of course, we feared that the instrument had been completely ruined, but, strange to say, it was little the worse for its experience.

My house shopping in any event would be meager, not only because of the scarcity of merchandise from which to select, but anything worth while cost more than a lieutenant's pay could afford. My curtains were of unbleached muslin, trimmed with strips of the same material that Annie Yates had dyed red with beet juice, and when they were completed they were a work of art. Charlotte Moylan and Mrs. Custer undertook to make a rug, and by the time it was finished every woman in the garrison had had a hand in it, so it was really the work of a regimental union.

As for the rug itself, its center was cut out of some old army-blue trousers of General Custer and Captain Moylan stitched cleverly together and edged with discarded yellow trouser stripes, and on the very end came a border of my crepe mourning veil, "to give it character," explained Mrs. Custer. The combination sounds like the nightmare of a cheese addict, but really it was most effective and colorful. It was most impractical, we all admitted, but then it was only to be used on state occasions and placed where it would not be heavily trod on. The back foundation consisted of an old army blanket, doubled, to give it body.

"Oh," I exclaimed rapturously, "it's exquisite."

"It might have come from France," commented Mrs. Custer, "as far as the delicate coloring is concerned."

"Yes," agreed Annie contemplatively, "or even Italy, with its blue center."

"And," chimed in Maggie Calhoun, "that little bit of orange contributed by Charlotte Moylan gives it just a touch of orientalism, don't you think?"

And so we played at make-believe in order to camouflage the real conditions.

Maggie was now busy with the muslin again, making a sizable closet-door bag. "For your shoes, my dear," she explained. "You simply can't leave them on the floor or you will be putting your feet into icebergs this winter."

Time wore on. I received a letter from Frank written from camp on the Cheyenne River, saying that since it would probably be still some weeks before he could join me, I had better be thinking of returning to Rice, for after the middle of August we might expect snow. I was to remain with Mrs. Benteen until his return, but the quarters that had been assigned us would be ready for occupancy at any time. Furthermore, we had been assured that all the ranking out for the season had been about completed, so I need not be uneasy. There was an army custom in those days that permitted a ranking officer, should he prefer the quarters of a subaltern, to take them over for his own use. This was being done constantly and accepted good-naturedly as a military regulation, and was known as "ranking out," and often ranker and ousted one might be the best of friends.

While I was still at Lincoln, Lieutenant Calhoun's troop, then in the field, was transferred from Rice to Lincoln, and of course Maggie was radiant with joy at the prospect of being stationed at Headquarters with her brothers, but how little we know of destiny's planning!

One day as I dropped in at the Custers' as usual, I glimpsed the General sitting in a side room, wearing what appeared to be an encompassing bib. Behind him stood a company barber trimming his hair, and as the curls fell upon a sheet stretched

on the floor I was moved to remark enviously,
"What a pity to waste such curls on a mere man."

He laughed, his eyes twinkling as he retorted
teasingly, "Why grudge mere man a little bit of
embellishment?"

Later he appeared on the porch with three small
boxes which he tendered, one by one, to Annie
Yates, Mrs. Custer, and me.

"Lest I should be labeled stingy," he stated with
mock solemnity.

In each box reposed a single golden curl. Of
course, this provoked much hilarity, in which he
joined heartily. I slipped my gift in my pocket
and forgot about it until some years later when it
served me in an odd capacity.

As Maggie was anxious to transfer her household goods, such as they were, from Fort Rice to
Lincoln, we started together for the former post
—she to leave there forever, and I to establish my
first army home.

Curiously enough, the rain that had been so
niggardly all summer poured in bucketfuls, and the
wind blew so cold that we huddled gratefully under
a robe.

Mrs. Benteen—bless her!—was delighted to see
me and, with the other women of the post, helped
me to get our rickety old quarters ready for occupancy. How to make them habitable was the problem, because as the government had decided to
abandon this post in the near future, nothing had
been done to improve them, and with doors, windows, and floors warped almost into sluices, I had

to invent stopgaps. So we packed the floor cracks with strips of gunny sack, and tacked folds of it under the door edges to keep out the cold, and the quartermaster made me some narrow, removable pieces of wood to prevent the windows from rattling and to keep out the elements as well. Mrs. Hart kindly brought over a lot of old *Army and Navy Journals* to cover the walls, but I preferred strips of worn canvas. I had brought some bright calico to tack on boxes that served as seats, and I had even edged some army blankets used for floor coverings with the same, and it really gave the place quite an air. Our army cots also bloomed with calico spreads, and the quartermaster made me a dining-room table from bits of all kinds of wood and stained it mahogany. Of course, the huge, wood-burning stoves were eyesores, but this couldn't be helped. My kitchen utensils were of the crudest—a few iron skillets, tin cups, and dippers. Our crockery was plain white, and heavy, but at least it was strong—very different from the delicate china to which I had been accustomed. Yet I was as happy as a lark because, crude as everything was in the house, it was my own, and I didn't have to sit gingerly on an antique chair belonging to some ancestor for fear of breaking it, but I could plump myself down on my covered-box furniture in comfort. When Maggie Calhoun ran over to say good-by, her eyes dancing with anticipation of a jolly winter at Headquarters, I didn't feel so depressed after all, because my little nest did look attractive, and, with my colored Lizzie in the kitchen, I awaited impatiently the return of the troops.

A few days after my arrival I saw a tall, slender figure, in a uniform so new that the buttons and shoulder straps gleamed like gold in the sun, go streaking across the parade ground, and, as I gazed on the West Point set of his back, I called to Mrs. Benteen, sitting on her porch.

"I see that Jack Sturgis has joined for duty."

"Yes," she flashed back, "he applied for his father's regiment."

During one of the early chill spells in September I was about to stretch myself and yawn when something caught my eyes, and I sat bolt upright instead. My incredulous gaze beheld a long rattlesnake undulating across the floor toward the stove, and in its wake followed a retinue of offspring. Evidently the reptiles had been hibernating somewhere under the rotting old floor, and the quiet warmth of the room had lured them from their nest. Locked in horror for a few seconds, I sat stone still, for my unwelcome visitors were sprawled between me and both dining-room and hall doors. But here the instinct of self-preservation twanged sharply on my mental wires, and I came alive again. I had learned the lesson of vibratory effect on reptiles, so I cautiously lifted my feet to the rounds of my chair and, leaning toward the low window, raised it noiselessly, quickly, and literally hurled my ninety-two pounds of being through it and onto the porch, where I carefully and swiftly closed the sash before the draught could disturb the rattlers, then ran around the back to the kitchen.

On the stove stood a cauldron of boiling water, and Lizzie was in the act of placidly sorting over some soiled linen, but it slipped from her hands when she saw my face.

"Listen," I whispered, "the living room is full of snakes, and if they get away they'll keep coming back and we'll never feel safe."

She looked at me tolerantly. "Honey," she asked, "has you de fever?"

"No, no," I answered impatiently, "come and see."

She opened the door slightly and peered in, then tiptoed back to me.

"Now, Missy," she commanded, "you stay outta this and leave everything to Lizzie," and, being a coward, I gladly complied. Back to the porch I scampered, my teeth chattering from cold and excitement, and watched the colored woman enter the living room in her stocking feet—shoes were too noisy—holding a pair of long kitchen tongs. The warmth of the stove after the biting cold beneath the floor must have lulled the reptiles into heavy drowsiness, for they all remained inert as the woman stealthily approached them. Suddenly the tongs flashed and caught the big mother snake at the back of the head, and with it writhing in the cold clutch of metal she carried it out. Each of the young ones suffered the same fate, and when the last one disappeared I returned to the room, chilled to the bone, and hugged the fire.

"What did you do with them?" I inquired.

"Jess threw 'em into de boiling clothes pan," she replied cheerfully.

"Oh," I cried with relief, "then they're definitely dead."

"Yas'um, dey suttenly is dead," she assured me with a chuckle.

At lunchtime I sat down at the table ready for a cup of steaming coffee and perhaps some creamed chipped beef, instead of which was set before me a platter of something else, surrounded by strips of bacon.

"What's this, Lizzie?" I asked.

"Jess de snakes."

"Snakes!" I exclaimed, pushing the platter away. "I couldn't touch them."

"But dey's mighty good eatin'," she pleaded. "My sixth husband down in Kansas always 'lowed dey was as good as chicken."

"Take them away," I insisted, "and bring me something else."

Here the cold air blew through the rooms, and I heard the front door bang. "Anyone home?" called the cheery voice of Jack Sturgis, stamping his boots noisily.

"Come in," I urged, "and have a cup of coffee and some snake meat."

"Snake meat," he echoed incredulously, "at this time of year?"

"Yes, sir." I told my story.

"Snake meat—will I have some? Just watch me," and he plumped himself down at the table.

I pushed my own plate and the platter over toward him.

"Where's your plate?" he wanted to know.

"I wouldn't touch the stuff," I declared disgustedly.

"Nonsense. Did you ever eat it?"

I shook my head, and Lizzie, hovering by the door, explained plaintively, "I done tole her, Lieutenant Jack, dat it was as good as chicken."

"Better," he vowed, and, reaching for my fork, he pronged a small piece of meat. "Here—taste it."

"No," I stated firmly with a grimace of distaste as I watched him relish what he had on his own plate.

A pause. Then he resumed, "You know, you're unique in your line."

"Really?" I beamed, as pleased as a flattered child.

"Yes. You're the only army woman I know who hasn't the nerve to try a little snake meat."

The red flamed under my skin, and the taunt whipped my pride.

"I'm not afraid," I defied him, "but I just don't fancy it."

"That's your excuse," he scoffed, and began waving the piece on my fork back and forth. I was so nettled that I leaned over, grabbed it, and put it in my mouth. Um—not so bad—in fact, it was good, very good, and right here I know that rascal winked at Lizzie, for with alacrity she appeared with a fresh plate, which she put at my place. And do you believe it, the two of us ate that entire platter of snakes!

Well, that was the time I did the biting, but a week later I had a curious experience. It was my habit, when I was alone at night, to keep a kerosene light burning, for the Indians were passing the stockade by the hundreds both day and night, and all the force we had to protect us was just a handful of men. Of course, a lamp wouldn't have done a particle of good if they had seen fit to attack us, but its glow was a comfort to me. On this particular occasion I had retired early, and it seemed to me that I had hardly fallen asleep when I was awakened suddenly by a sharp, stabbing pain in my thumb. I turned up the wick just in time to see a rat scuttle from under my covers, and my hand was full of blood. Since I was young and healthy, a thorough cleansing in cold water and a bandage were sufficient to prevent infection, but to this day—and I am a great-grandmother—I still carry two tiny white scars on my thumb where I was bitten by that rodent long ago.

But to return to Jack Sturgis. What a boon that youngster proved to be to dead old Fort Rice! Army bred, nothing was a trouble to him, nothing too uncomfortable, and he took his hardships with a laugh.

Often during the terrific winter that followed, when in hip buffalo boots, I sat huddled round the old stove that was white hot on your face while your back froze, Jack would breeze in, his handsome face ruddy from the cold, and remark playfully, "Heavens, how can you stand such heat— I'm melting," and would try to laugh me out of my congealed misery.

Yes, Jack Sturgis was one of the most lovable boys who ever came out of the United States Military Academy, and after the Custer Massacre his seat at the bachelors' mess was always left vacant. As for me and those who knew him, even today we cannot speak of him without tears filling our eyes.

On October 7, with the snow knee deep, the troops returned. I was all excitement and anticipation, but when a brawny man with a heavy beard suddenly opened the front door and caught me in his arms I hauled off and struck him a blow in the face that almost staggered him. At this a ringing laugh boomed forth, and, contrite, I recognized my husband. He was thrilled with the "beauty" of the place. How little it took in those days to make us happy! How little—and yet, when I look around today and note the luxury of the modern army post, I wonder if we old army pioneers hadn't something very dear that the service will never know again.

There was snow, eternal snow, from September until June, one storm piling upon another. We walked between paths of ploughed snow, the walls so high that we could scarcely see over them. The stark white required goggles to prevent snow blindness, and the air was dry and rarefied.

People went about their duties like wraiths, for no footfall fell upon the ear, because this huge cushion of snow muffled all sounds and brought about the stillness of death. We had no church, no music, no entertainments, and we read and re-read the same old books and papers over and over again. We didn't even go outside the stockade without escort for fear of the Indians.

We knew that in summer we would be fighting mosquitoes, yet as soon as the snow melted we were contented, after the severe winter, making a home for our husbands who had to spend so many months away.

The great event of the day was the arrival of the mail from Bismarck, twenty-five miles over-land, the same ambulance returning next day through violent snowstorms, sometimes unable to penetrate the canyons at all, when turned into swollen streams. What a contrast to the winter before spent in the South!

Of course, I surrounded myself with as many souvenirs of my old home as I could, and some-times when I felt homesick among those hum-mocks of snow, I used to open my family album and look upon the sweet face of my lady-mother and other dear ones. It seemed to bring them nearer to me. One day I was thus engaged when two little children of the garrison came to visit me. It happened that I had opened the book at a photo-graph of my father, taken just before he died, and he looked very ill. Outside of cowboys, neither of my visitors had even seen a civilian before, and the small Hart boy, pointing to the picture, asked, "Who's he?"

"My father," I replied.

"Where is he?"

"He's dead."

"Who killed him?" demanded the boy. It was a perfectly natural question, for no one died a natural death out there, but was killed either by Indians, or in barroom brawls, or frozen to death.

"Nobody killed him," I assured him.

Both he and his companion looked puzzled for a moment, then the little girl piped up. "Nobody killed him," she repeated. "He just died his own self."

Christmas on the Prairie Frontier

xvi

WITH THE APPROACH of roaring December my husband and I decided to give a Christmas tree party at our quarters on Christmas Eve, but where to find either tree or trimmings was the problem. The trader's store offered a meager assortment of articles, and the commissary could supply only such staples as sugar, coffee, flour, and other simple necessities. However, soldiers were sent out to scour the neighborhood for anything that looked like a tree and finally returned with some forlorn bunches of squatty sage and cedar brush. The outlook was discouraging, but it stimulated imagination, and we started to fashion something that at least resembled a tree. We hung the plants in relays from the ceiling down to within a few feet of the floor, and beneath them was placed a wash-tub decorated with gaily painted paper and filled with sand and whatever crude presents the town of Bismarck afforded. A sort of Christmas pie idea. So far so good, but now for the trimmings, and in this paper played the most conspicuous part. Paints were produced and brushes wielded, while plain paper took on startling colors, and scissors were busy cutting yards and yards into strips, which served as festoons or were converted into cornucopias to be filled with homemade candy.

Some thrifty soul had garnered a few nuts, and these were dexterously covered with silver foil salvaged from cigars and then hung upon the tree along with ancient Christmas cards, resurrected from trunks, and tied with scraps of faded ribbon which had been ironed and freshened.

Jack Sturgis and some other youngsters just out of the Point displayed hidden artistic talents. They colored candles bright red, cut them in two, and perched them jauntily on the branches. They fashioned a huge paper bell, also painted red, pasting on the edges cut-out pictures of Santa Claus, and when the work was completed the ensemble stood forth as a thing of beauty.

The refreshments would be sandwiches, cake, and candy, lemonade made from the usual citric acid crystals, and, of course, ice cream evolved from condensed milk, whipped-up gelatine, and the whites of eggs. The eggs by the way, wrapped in cotton, were brought from Bismarck by the mailman, who, to keep such precious articles from freezing, always carried them inside his buckskin shirt, against his bare breast.

Christmas Eve dawned bright and clear, and the temperature had moderated. Someone brought an old banjo, another had unearthed an antique guitar, another a jew's-harp. With such dance music provided we swung into the Virginia Reel with much merriment, and then the old square dances had their turn. What a beautiful time we had! Finally, before midnight, Lieutenant Gibson, being Officer of the day, had to make his rounds of the outposts, and shortly afterwards the party broke up, everyone tired but happy.

When the last guest had departed, I thought I would take a peep into the kitchen, now dark and deserted, so, with lighted candle held high, I opened the door. As the flame stabbed through the blackness I suddenly gasped and gazed before me with startled eyes, for on the side porch appeared some strangers huddled together—strangers of juvenile stature, one barely tall enough to see above the window casement. In short, my uninvited guests were small Indian children, who were staring through the glass at the tree in mesmeric entrancement. For a moment I was held spellbound in surprise, then, cautiously, so as not to frighten them, I opened the porch door and motioned them to enter. At first they cowered and shrank away, then a straight-backed youngster in buckskin, dragging by the hand a diminutive squaw about four years old, stepped into the room, the others following warily, single file. How had they gained entrance to the garrison, I wondered? Then I recalled a slight breach in the stockade wall, just big enough to admit the wriggling in and out of one small body at a time.

I turned to the supposed leader of the party and, speaking slowly, asked, pointing to the tree, "Someone tell Indian boy about it?"

He nodded, as the little hostiles around the agencies picked up a smattering of English very quickly.

"Who tell Indian boy?"

"Horn Toad."

Horn Toad was a good-natured Indian scout, adored by all the children in the garrison.

"Oh," I nodded, while the little frozen band huddled about the stove in stolid silence, "and who is she?" indicating the wee squaw.

"Sister," replied the boy, while the little girl clung more fiercely to his hand. My eyes ran over the tiny figure, and my heart contracted. The poor tot shivered and drew across the shoulders of her calico dress an impromptu shawl made of gunny sack, and a strip of the same material served as her only headgear. Her moccasins and leggings were of buckskin. The young warriors were clad in whole suits of it, but, evidently, when it came to the females of the species, the supply had given out. It was a miracle that the little band hadn't been frozen to death.

Just how, where, or why at this season of the year these people were abroad instead of being under shelter at the agencies did not matter. The fact remained that they and at least some of their tribe had set up their wickiups somewhere near by. I mentally shook myself. What an unconscionable hour for these children to be up. They must be returned to their mothers at once, and yet, as I looked into their timid, expectant faces, pity stirred within me, and my logic went woefully awry. Heaven only knew how long they had waited out there in the cold, feasting their eyes upon this glittering paradise, and that set me thinking. Quickly I drew them into the living room and towards the Christmas tree pie, which, I was confident, still held a few treasures, and, digging into the sand myself, I fished out a Jack-in-the-box which I presented to the little lady. Her black eyes leaped with surprise and joy, and her wee hands trembled as she clutched the toy. Then, making a motion for them to continue, I flew to the kitchen to heat up what cocoa still remained. The striker was just leaving for his barracks when I called to him.

"Oh, Alkorn," I instructed, "go to the nearest bastion and tell the sentinel to relay to other sentinels that, in the event of any Indians hanging around and looking for children, they are at Lieutenant Gibson's quarters and will be along soon."

During my absence my guests had certainly explored the entire contents of the tub. The appearance of the Jack-in-the-box had dissipated their last vestige of hesitation, and they plunged feverishly into the sand, and with each rag doll, toy pistol, or other treasure exhumed, they became in fact wild Indians—wild with delight— the boys voicing their emotions in short grunts, the wee one in squeals of rapture.

It was upon this scene of oozing, scattering sand that I entered, bearing a pot of steaming cocoa, but the children refused to abandon the magic tub until the very last toy had been salvaged. Then they drank long and thirstily of the refreshing beverage, and soon color returned to their pinched cheeks and warmth crept back into their little chilled fingers. Noting all this, I communed with myself thoughtfully. I should have sent them home right away, I told myself severely, yet I continued to heap their laps with goodies, popcorn, nuts, and candy. Besides, there was some ice cream left over and cake, too, that were begging to be eaten, and what was a party without them? So, before they knew it, mounds of pink and white concoction were whisked in front of the little savages, who immediately plunged small eager fingers into the pretty, fluffy stuff, only to recoil from the sudden chill. The tiny squaw was the first to experiment with it, by cautiously licking some off her palm, and her cherubic smile would have inspired a masterpiece from Raphael. They needed no further urging and attacked the ice cream, stuffing themselves with all the abandon of healthy, hungry children.

While they were thus engaged, I ran upstairs looking for old blankets, woolen stockings, and socks. I found a short coat of my own, some mittens and galoshes and warm mufflers. Suddenly queer sounds coming from below sent me scurrying halfway downstairs, where I paused. The noise started with the clapping of hands, accompanied by a weird chant. This was followed by the sound of softly muffled feet and short, sharp whoops, at first faint but growing louder and louder. I sank upon the stairs and peered through the bannisters into the living room, and what I beheld kept me rooted to the spot. My eyes dilated before a picturesque phase of barbaric expression.

The straight-backed boy, evidently wishing to

do his part and that of his tribe toward the entertainment, was staging a performance of his own and was directing the others in some kind of dance. One boy and the diminutive squaw stood at the side clapping their hands and chanting monotonously, the latter moving her hips and body in imitation of the older squaws while, circling the stove in single file, the young braves stamped upon the carpet with the firmness of buffaloes combined with the whirlwind lightness of the wildcat, their lithe frames swaying like the prairie grasses and with a rhythm as perfect as a set measure. Backwards and forwards they flung themselves as though made of elastic rubber, bending pliant heads and necks and emitting long-drawn-out whoops of joy. The crunching into the carpet of ruinous sand mattered not, for on the step I sat like petrified wood, lost in wonder at the wild beauty and cadence of that native dance. Why, I pondered, did white children have to spend money to attain anything like the grace of these aborigines to whom it seemed as inborn and as natural as a spring of cool, pure water. The dirge changed, and the little redskins swung into close, group formation, each executing fast, fantastic steps. Followed more insistent hand clapping and droning. The young bucks quickly flung back into single file, whereupon the dance became fiercer, the whoops louder and longer, and with a frenzy that almost shook the floor they fairly leaped about the stove until the leader held up his hand and stopped. The droning ceased, the embryo braves threw themselves, gasping, upon the carpet, and the wee one slid down beside the young chief.

I drew a deep breath, hurried back upstairs, and brought down an armful of clothing and blankets. Then I bundled up the wee squaw like a bale of cotton, tied my too-big mittens on her warm little hands, and gave the rest of the blankets, mufflers, and galoshes to the boys. After that I stripped the tree of its remaining gifts, put candy and cake in a bag, which I consigned to the care of the straight-backed boy, and very reluctantly let my guests out again into the night. I glanced up at the clock in the hall. Already it was Christmas. The snow crunched crisply beneath light retreating steps while again and again the happy children, clutching their cherished toys, turned radiant faces over their shoulders for one last look and smile.

Finally, the small, straight-backed Indian boy, bringing up the rear with his Christmas burdens, patted his mouth with his slim hand and emitted the farewell call of his tribe, which seemed to linger on the air even after the little band had faded from view.

I smiled to myself, blew out the kerosene lamp in the hall, and trudged wearily upstairs while, drifting through the still, approaching dawn and echoing from bastion to bastion, came the comforting call of the sentinels, "One o'clock and all's well."

Winter—1876

xvii

JANUARY, 1876, was ushered in by a howling blizzard, so violent that sentinels atop the bastions had to be relieved every hour. In fact, there were instances when they were blown bodily right off their posts, and landed in the deep, sand-dry snow. We were literally prisoners of the elements, frozen in for the winter, and locked as securely within those stockade walls as though confined behind iron bars. When the wailing of the wind ceased for a day or two the garrison was blanketed with the stillness of death, the snow so deep that even foot-padding became noiseless. The winter had been unusually severe, and many discharged soldiers, who had found that land could be bought for a song and had acquired ranches, became disheartened with the heavy mortality among their cattle. These men with the other settlers endured untold hardships, and those of us living in the stockade helped them all we could, especially the army surgeons. The latter faced death many times in the blizzards to reach sufferers in illness and childbirth. They went out of their line of governmental duty, without one thought of monetary compensation.

One surgeon, amputating the leg of a ranchman, lost three fingers from gangrene. Certainly these pioneer good samaritans deserved as much credit for the safety and physical comforts of the settlers as the men who did the actual fighting.

Inside the rickety quarters we piled the stoves with cedar and cottonwood, so green that while one end burned, sap ran out at the other. Along Officers' Row we managed to eke out some measure of relaxation among ourselves, but the enlisted men gave us cause for anxiety. This was years before the general installment of gymnasiums and other forms of amusement, and something had to be done to keep them from brooding or fighting among themselves. Finally, Jack Sturgis evolved the idea of converting the sawmill into an impromptu theater, where the soldiers could give benefit performances to raise funds for the purchase of a billiard table and a bowling alley. The price of admission was to be twenty-five cents, and all hands and the cook turned out to contribute to the worthy cause. The soldiers themselves greeted the proposition enthusiastically, and it was really surprising how well they could act. In fact, one man in the infantry played his roles so intelligently that he became imbued with the idea that he possessed unsuspected histrionic talents. He began to act on the slightest provocation, and when, during sentry duty, it was necessary to call out the hours, he did so in deep, stentorian tones, adding with a flourish, "And all is well, my lord."

As the winter waned, my husband began to worry at the thought of leaving me almost unprotected during the approaching summer campaign.

He urged me to return East for a while, but this I promptly vetoed. Not only would I be so far away from him, but we really couldn't afford such a trip.

The Indians were constantly passing back and forth to join larger forces in the north, so the sentinels were ever vigilant, watching for surprise attacks. No Indian, not even a scout, was permitted to pass through the fort, except by command of the guard.

The summer previous, while the cavalry was out on a campaign, a band of hostiles halted just at the entrance of the stockade. A new recruit, on sentry duty, fearing they might force their way through and with only thirty soldiers left to guard the garrison, fired his gun. Always alert to sound alarms, each man sprang for his firearms, and the women were ordered indoors.

An infantry captain, highest in rank, took command. He happened to be shaving at the time, but he buckled on his cartridge belt, grabbed his carbine, and rushed out just as he was, his face covered with lather. He climbed the bastion and started to orate to the Indians. Suddenly one redskin pointed to the officer's face and began to laugh, followed by another and another until finally the whole band was tittering, even the soldiers, and lastly the captain himself.

This broke the strain, the Indians passed on, and the garrison resumed its usual calm.

There was but one cemetery, on a hill just outside the fort, which accommodated not only the

white men but some Indians as well. The bodies of
the latter were wrapped in buffalo robes, then lifted
and placed upon a sort of skin canopy which was
stretched across two high poles. Food was deposited there for the dead up in the Happy Hunting
Ground. This, of course, the birds ate or buzzards
destroyed, notwithstanding the Indians often came
back to replenish the larder.

Captain Verling Hart had a little child temporarily buried there, expecting to take the body East
when he could obtain leave of absence. In the interim, Mrs. Hart made many sad pilgrimages to
the little mound. On one of these occasions some
children joined her in her walk there, and they
were all busy weeding and planting flowers on the
grave. Suddenly, out of the corner of her eye, Mrs.
Hart saw something moving behind a tombstone.
Long, bronzed fingers curled around the stained,
crude monument, and, rising gradually to his full
six feet, an Indian appeared in complete war
raiment, paint and all. From his feathered war
bonnet, which hung loosely down his bare back, to
the menacing tomahawk worn at his side, he presented a terrifying spectacle.

For a moment sheer terror gripped the woman.
Except for herself, this hostile Indian, and her
small charges, the prairie was utterly deserted.
It was needless to scream, for there was not a soul
to hear her. She and her little ones were completely at the mercy of this savage. There was but one
thing to do—ignore him. So she continued her
work quietly, begging the children to show no fear.

Walking with the usual upright carriage of the
Indian, the brave approached her and began to talk
in sign language. How many papooses? She answered the number on her fingers. He pointed to
the little grave, then to her. "Your papoose?" he
asked. She nodded, gave the little mound a final
pat, rose from her knees, and started for the post,
the children, white-faced, following behind her.
The Indian fell into step beside her, and together
they crossed the prairie.

Finally they reached the very gate of the stockade. The sentinels stood spellbound at the sight.
She waited a moment, but as her escort made no
move to leave her, she nodded to the soldier on the
bastion. Still amazed, he slowly swung open the
portal. Through it passed the officer's wife, her
brood, and the big Indian. The men were in barracks or on the range at the time, but the women,
sewing or reading on their porches, were held
speechless with stunned surprise as they gaped at
her and the magnificent savage, who followed her
straight to Captain Hart's quarters. Here she motioned him to wait on the porch while she went
inside. The table was set for lunch, so she grabbed
a plateful of food and took it out to him. Then,
returning to the dining room, she promptly fainted.
Both the captain and the doctor were summoned.
The guards were ordered to search for the brave,
but Mrs. Hart opposed this move. She stated that
the man had not harmed her in any way, but
rather, had shown her great respect and kindness.
Perhaps if anything were done to injure him, it

might precipitate an uprising. She could have had him stopped at the gate but considered it wiser to act just as she had done.

In the meantime, the Indian had faded away and was never heard from again.

About this time an officer at Lincoln was assigned for duty at Washington. This, of course, left a vacancy at Lincoln. General Custer wrote to my husband asking him if he would like to be transferred and join him.

This was welcome news, because going to regimental headquarters meant, in a measure, the end of our isolation. Not only would it give us additional social pleasure from both cavalry and infantry posts with the conveniences of Bismarck so near, but to my husband it spelled security for me against the Indians during the coming summer, while he would be away on the campaign. Furthermore, Mollie and Donald were returning from the South, our many, many friends were there, and we would have the joy of hearing the regimental band. The proposition sounded ideal. We were naturally elated and were the envy of those left in the stockade. However, the usual amount of red tape had to be enforced. Papers were sent through the regiment to the War Department, which took time before the transfer could be accomplished, and the final signature of my husband was required.

I fairly trod on eggshells those days and had already begun to assemble my personal belongings for packing. The post office was at the trader's store, and there Frank finally received the im-

portant letter. I shall never forget that day as long
as I live, because it began and ended so differently
from what I had expected. I can see my happy
soldier standing with ruddy, beaming face in the
doorway.

"Here it is!" he cried exultantly. "Just my signature, and we can start packing at once." And
laughingly he tossed me the document.

And here I experienced the most peculiar sensation of my whole life. I had been just as enthusiastic as he over the transfer; even more so, because
of the many benefits I would enjoy. Everything
seemed so hopeful and happy with Mrs. Custer's
affectionate letter of welcome in my pocket; yet,
as that envelope fell into my lap, something happened to me. A sudden chill swept over my heart
like the touch of cold, invisible fingers, and a curious foreboding enveloped me. I tried to shake it
off, but my face must have registered an unusual
expression, because Frank asked quickly, "What's
the matter? News been too much for you?"

I nodded and attempted a smile. We went into
lunch—lunch which I could not eat. He, however,
was in high spirits—planning, planning for the
future—as I smiled my set smile. Curiously
enough, memory of that night when I had seen the
huge Indian village and had thought irrelevantly
of Donald swam again in my head. It was all so
inexplicable, so silly, I told myself angrily—yet
that sinister brooding bit deeper and deeper into
my being.

After lunch my husband ran gaily to his desk

and picked up a pen. "Guess I'll sign this now and mail it."

But here a compelling force ran through me like quicksilver, an indefinable something which forbade the signing of that paper. I found myself suggesting, "Why hurry? Wait until tonight."

I was playing for time—time to analyze and combat this strange mood that had settled on me. He hesitated a moment, played with the pen, dropped it, and strode out of the room whistling, banging the door behind him.

I sighed with relief; it seemed like a reprieve, and in order to keep up my courage I started to hum while I dug into my bureau drawers, picking out certain articles for special packing.

All that afternoon I struggled with that weird something that had gripped me, almost physically; that had tried to rob us of our wonderful opportunity. But it refused to be dislodged and clung like the tentacles of some strange animal all day —all night.

"Stupid—stupid," I accused myself fiercely, thrusting aside the fact that certain strange premonitions had guided our lady-mother through some critical moments of her life. But I wasn't beaten yet, I told myself stubbornly—we wanted that transfer too desperately. Therefore, after hours of this internal turmoil, I was surprised to feel tears dropping on my hands, and I realized that I was crying softly—crying because I knew that I would have to dash all our hopes to the ground, and that, for some obscure reason, which only my dear God knew, my husband must *not* join Custer's personal command.

After dinner Frank went to his desk and picked up the pen again, saying, "Well, let's get this over with."

Here I rose, quivering, and slipped my hand over his.

"No, Frank," I pleaded, "please don't sign that paper."

He whirled and, taking me by the shoulders, looked searchingly into my face.

"What's really the matter with you?" he demanded anxiously. "You've been acting strangely all day. Are you ill?"

"No," I replied. Taking a quick hitch in my unsteady voice, I resumed, "You won't understand, but something is hammering at my brain, warning me not to let you accept this transfer."

"Ridiculous," he scoffed. "Why, Custer will think me a vacillating fool. Come, be reasonable."

But I shook my head helplessly. He argued with me in vain. It was for my own security and his peace of mind, but whatever power enthralled me held me like a vise. With tears raining down my face I finally blurted out, "Oh, please, please, don't let us talk any more! Write Custer that you've changed your mind!"

He was silent for a moment, and then said, "I won't sign this tonight, but tomorrow you will be over your attack of nerves and will feel differently."

At this point the bugle sounded for tattoo.

Snatching up his belt and saber, he crossed the room, saying as he banged the door, "I'll be damned if I can understand women!"

Being Officer of the day, he did not return until after his midnight rounds were over. When he came in I feigned sleep which was far from my eyelids. In fact, I lay staring all night, the finger on my heart now weighing like a piece of lead. By morning my swollen face and eyes decried any kinship to the supposed dauntless wife of a soldier.

Frank took one look at me, then with a heavy heart returned the papers to Custer—unsigned. Immediately, the finger was lifted from my heart, and I went back, happily, to the humdrum, narrow life of that little stockade post. Thank God I did heed that warning, for two months later, when the entire regiment marched to the valley of the Little Bighorn, Frank was still with the command of the level-headed Benteen; but that is another story.

Colonel Benteen and my husband were ordered to a reservation down the river to investigate some Indian trouble. While they were away Benteen's youngest child died, and I was with the poor mother every moment I could spare. No coffins were obtainable, not even a carpenter, so a soldier just put together a plain pine box, the best he could do—but, oh, how forlorn! Mrs. Benteen asked me if it would be possible to line it so as to take away some of the crudeness. During the short span of my army life I had been forced to do many things, but this seemed tempting the impossible

even had I known how, as there was no material
to be had, for love or money.

"This must be finished tonight, so do try to bring
it to me, no matter how late," she said.

I hurried hopefully to the trader's store, but
found nothing among the flyspecked, shopworn
goods; dejectedly I returned home. I looked among
my own belongings in vain, and then I had an idea.
Going to a certain trunk, I reverently lifted a well-
covered package and untied it. Again my wedding
dress looked up at me, after months of retirement.
It was lovely, and my choicest treasure, but it
had to be sacrificed. Armed with a big bundle
of cotton batting from the hospital, and a box of
tacks, I was ready to begin my task as soon as the
casket arrived, about nine o'clock in the evening.
Not having a table big enough, I placed all my
things on the floor and there started my work. I
padded the inside and the lid, then covered it all
with soft satin pleating. The swan's-down was to
be used for a pillow upon which to rest the baby's
head, but try as I did, I could not hide the black
heads of the tacks. It was almost midnight, and
all was deathly still. Suddenly, I was roused by
a man's voice at the open window.

"What are you doing at this hour of the night?"

Startled, I glanced up and saw Lieutenant
Mathey.

"Being Officer of the day," he explained, "and
seeing your light burning while all the other quarters were dark, I came over to investigate."

When I told him of the troublesome tacks, the

Frenchman pondered a moment, then suggested, "It is possible that I may find something for you at my quarters which may answer."

And sure enough, he returned with a box of white-headed tacks, just the thing required. It was said of him (while he was campaigning with pack horses or mules, carrying only a few pounds of luggage) that he was always able to produce extra corks for the canteens, a little liquor or tobacco, though he himself neither smoked nor drank. He would bring them along for the convenience of of his friends.

We finished the casket, and it was my belief that angels could have done no more. It was almost dawn, and with the finished article under his arm, Lieutenant Mathey escorted me to Colonel Benteen's quarters.

At the funeral there was neither service nor clergyman. We walked to the little cemetery on the hill, knelt beside the small grave, and commended the baby's soul to the Father whence it came.

During the winter there had been marked unrest among the Indians. The Sioux, a warlike nation, scorned the confines of agencies and camped about in the buffalo country. However, they did go to the reservations to visit friends and relatives, and here they conducted themselves with arrogance and fomented discord.

Sitting Bull, an Uncpapa Sioux chief, made his huge camp a rendezvous, not only for the Indians from the agencies when they hunted for meat and

robes, but for representatives of the different
Sioux tribes: the Cheyenne, Arapaho, and others.
These people were known as hostile. Many of them
were renegade outlaws, and upon these the stocky
forty-two-year-old chief, acting as lavish host,
prodded their hatred for the white man.

He was not a warrior chief. An Indian scout
has described him: "He was a great coward and
a very great liar—a big head and little heart." In
battle he took no part, but, serpent-wise, remained
in the village "making medicine," and predicted
that the soldiers would attack and be killed by
overwhelming numbers of redskins.

Minor cases of misdeeds by the Indians the
soldiers overlooked, but when they started to com-
mit serious depredations on the commerce and
railroads of the country, and murdered women
and children, the government at Washington determined that these criminals should be brought
to justice, and the rest of the savages confined
within the agencies.

Learning of this ultimatum, Sitting Bull summoned all the tribes which paid him tribute.
Throughout the winter and spring months he had
assembled at his camp anywhere from twelve to
fifteen thousand warriors, all well equipped for
battle.

While the army men, through their scouts, were
not unaware of what was happening, and were preparing for a larger-manned and more vigorous
campaign, still they did not realize the number of
Indians about to take the warpath. All this wor-

ried Frank so much that I promised to join Mollie later in the summer, at Lincoln.

The late spring of 1876 had ended, and in a few weeks the troops would be on the march to Lincoln, there to be joined by the whole regiment, supplemented by some other commands under General Terry, and perhaps General Gibbon. In spite of the serious business ahead of them, everyone seemed happy at the prospect, anticipating the summer in the field, and feeling secure with such a large command. The grass was green where the snow had melted, and the meadow larks sang lustily. The boats were ploughing the river again, and everything was cheerful in that rarefied air, so light that one felt one could fly.

So the troops, in their wide-brimmed campaign hats and blue flannel shirts, marched away to the strains of "The Girl I Left Behind Me."

The night before their departure we had a gathering of the clan at our quarters, to say goodby. Jack Sturgis was not among us. Upon my husband's declining the Lincoln transfer, he had come springing over to our quarters, and with eyes shining had asked eagerly, "If you really don't want that transfer, Gib, do you mind if I take it?"

"Not at all, Jack," replied Frank promptly. "It will mean so much to you being at Lincoln with your parents."

"Yes, indeed," agreed the boy, his whole face lighting.

For one wild moment I wanted to put my hand

on his arm and plead, "Oh, don't do it, Jack; don't do it," but a warning glance from my husband checked the impulse. Besides, it wouldn't have done any good. The boy was too set upon it. Well, he had no difficulty in achieving the transfer, with General Sturgis' influence, and the day that he came to say good-by he was simply radiant with happiness. Poor, poor Jack!

The post was left with but a handful of infantry-men to guard it, some of whom were on the sick report. However, another company of infantry was on its way to us. A message brought by an Indian scout stated that the boat conveying it had stuck on a sand bar in the river. It did not arrive for two weeks.

We settled down patiently to wait for it. The sun did not set until nine o'clock, giving us a long twilight. Several friends had gathered on our porch, attracted by the music of my guitar, which I thought would cheer them up, when suddenly a shot rang out from the bastion, and a soldier came running to tell us that a large band of Indians were marching on the stockade. Terror spread through the garrison. I called frantically to my servants, but no one answered, and I found myself alone. I rushed upstairs for my revolver, and then, like an ostrich, I fell on my knees in a dark corner with my face to the wall and began to pray. I visioned Indians in war paint at my back until I heard the voice of my faithful Lizzie. She jerked me to my feet.

"Come on, honey," she said. "Dis ain't no time

to pray and be wastin' words, wid de Indians at de back door."

Then, seeing how frightened I was, she led me to a window overlooking the stockade.

"Dere dey goes, an' dey ain't tetched us," she soothed.

Sure enough, thousands of them were there with their squaws, children, and ponies. I pointed to the sudden flash of bright gleams in the moonlight as they trekked along.

"Guns," I murmured, and wondered where they got them, as the government had forbidden the post trader to sell firearms, ammunition, or whiskey on the reservation at Standing Rock. But it was the only place they could have bought them, and they were well supplied. Besides, their weapons were modern and not the old carbines used by the soldiers, which went bad after the second firing. Fortunately, the savages did not know of our helplessness, or I might not be here now telling the story. Though they were gone and out of sight, none of us slept a wink that night, fearing they might return and surprise us. We learned afterwards that they were on their way to join Sitting Bull, and then to massacre our command.

So life resumed its usual routine. We drifted day by day—waiting for what? During the regiment's sojourn at Lincoln, letters came from my husband telling of their joyous arrival there, and how disappointed General Custer was that Frank had decided against the transfer. Mrs. Custer had done her best to influence him in changing his

mind even then, and there was a wistful note in
the missives that made me feel very selfish. How
I did miss all the good times they were having
while waiting for the other commands from distant posts, and, apparently, every house seemed
to vie with each other in entertaining them. It
was as *Vanity Fair* says, "A sound of revelry by
night and brave men and fair women by day."

Well, thank heaven, they did have their last
fling of happiness, those youngsters, never dreaming of the Waterloo awaiting them, only a few
weeks away.

A scathing letter came also from Mollie, just
returned from the South with Donald. "My dear
little sister," she wrote, "have you lost your mind?
Do you realize what a position you have put poor
Frank in? The grief you have caused him and
his friends? As soon as the troops leave, I am going East to Mother, and you had better come with
me and then, when the men return in the autumn,
they can join us and we will take in the Centennial.
Your mind has become warped with the life of
depression you have led through fear at that Godforsaken post." Alas, poor Mollie, what overwhelming grief awaited her just a few weeks
ahead!

And now the troops were on the march, their
objective being Montana, where they would contact General Terry's command. Frank's letters
became less and less frequent, because of the increasing distance between us, but they were always cheerful and bore the tidings that there had

been no signs of Indians. The whole command was taking the adventure as a prolonged picnic, and these bits of news, brought by Indian scouts, were a great comfort to us all.

The Custer Massacre
xviii

SO TIME SLIPPED BY during the month of June. Our only pleasure after the torrid day was to gather on someone's porch in the long twilight, enjoy what little music we could muster, and try to forget our worries and the devilish mosquitoes. Many among us had sweet voices, and while I played the guitar everyone sang. One particular evening, early in July, we were singing "Annie Laurie," the war song of the Crimean War, and at the last verse:

> *"Go soldiers to your honored rest*
> *The bravest are the tenderest*
> *The loving and the daring,"*

we thought only of Balaklava, never realizing what the morrow's news would bring to us.

It was so stiflingly hot that we lingered on our porches until after tattoo. Then, glancing across the parade ground, we noticed small groups of soldiers talking excitedly together, and several people came running toward us, faces set and wild eyed.

One was Horn Toad, the Indian scout, who gasped in short, sharp sentences, "Custer killed. Whole command killed."

The guitar slipped from my knees to the floor,

the pink ball of knitting fell out of Charlotte Moylan's hands, rolling across the porch, the letter lying idly in Mrs. Benteen's lap fluttered over the rail and onto the parched lawn, and Mrs. de Rudio's sewing bag, containing the family mending, fell off the arm of her rocking chair with a thud.

White-lipped, we rose simultaneously, and Mrs. Benteen spoke, her voice trembling slightly in spite of herself, "How do you know, Horn Toad?"

"Speckled Cock, Indian scout, just come. Rode pony many miles. Pony tired. Indian tired. Say Custer shoot himself—at end. Say all dead."

Such tidings numbed us for a moment, but, remembering my husband's caution to believe no rumors unless officially confirmed, I cried huskily, "Oh, that's too sweeping, though there may have been a brush."

Why, our husbands were with Custer and also, we supposed, with the big command under Terry, so of course it couldn't be true, but the Indian shook his head vehemently, "Speckled Cock—good Indian—no lie," and he shot on by, leaving us as rigid as stone.

Finally, with the blood flowing back to our hearts again, we sat talking late into the night, stubbornly refusing to accept the Indian's statement.

Those of us without children dreaded going home, so I suggested that we all stick together for the rest of the night. Hence we remained at the quarters of Lieutenant de Rudio, whose wife put her brood to bed, then picked up all the pillows she could find and distributed them among us. Never will I forget that night. We settled ourselves to wait for morning, most of us lying on the floor, sleepless, only exchanging a word or two and springing up at every distant sound, thinking it might be a courier with messages. Otherwise, deathly silence encompassed us.

The moon cast its silver cover across our impromptu beds, bringing out the pallor of our faces and accentuating our wide, staring eyes. The minutes seemed like hours, while the occasional yapping of coyotes outside the stockade, combined with the chirping of crickets inside, broke the tense stillness from time to time and beat upon our ears like mournful portents. Gradually the night grew old, the moon cutting a trail across the faintly lightening sky, and we sat waiting— waiting.

Finally, just at daybreak, the whistle of a steamboat pierced the silence, as penetrating as a hunter's horn, and instantly we knew it brought news, good or bad. Unwashed, uncombed, the thud-thud of our hearts almost suffocating, we dashed to the trader-store post office, there to await the arrival of the dawdling old mailcoach. But even when our eager hands clutched our precious letters we were afraid to look at the dates, afraid to open them. However, it was with hysterical joy that I received two from Frank, one very brief, written immediately after the Massacre, simply announcing the tragedy, the other giving full particulars, penned nine days later. As

tears of thankfulness rolled down my cheeks, I
looked into the haggard faces of Mrs. Benteen,
Mrs. de Rudio, Mrs. Moylan, Mrs. Godfrey, Mrs.
Hart, and all the other patient, waiting women
connected with the expedition, and saw that they,
too, were weeping, quietly, reverently. All of those
from forlorn old Fort Rice were safely accounted
for—all but one, our dear Jack, so very young, so
beloved by us all. Had he never sought that fatal
transfer and remained with his troop, he too would
have returned alive. In spirit he was with us always, that merry, generous boy.

On the other hand, practically every house at
Lincoln was visited by death. Even my beloved
brother-in-law, Donald, of the big heart, was gone.

Here, for the sake of veracity, I quote the second
letter from my husband, written in pencil from the
battlefield, on government toilet paper.

Camp on the Yellowstone River,
Montana Territory,
July—4, 1876

My dear Wife—

We have just been notified that a mail will leave
at seven o'clock tonight, so I have time to write
you all the particulars.

We left the boat at the mouth of the Rosebud at
noon on the twenty-second. The boat came up the
mouth of the Big Horn with General Terry, and
crossed Gibbon's command which was to connect
with us on the Little Big Horn River. On the
twenty third, we struck an Indian trail, only two
days old, so we marched night and day at trot and
gallop with occasional short halts so, of course,

the men and horses became exhausted for the need of rest and food, but still we went pushing and crowding along. At ten/A/M, on the twenty-fifth we halted and officers call was sounded, and after we assembled, General Custer said the command had been discovered by the Indians, and our scout had reported the village about fifteen miles off. He then said that the companies would resume march in the order that the company commanders reported them ready. Well, as it happened, Benteen was the first to report, so when the forward call was sounded our H company was leading the column. As we marched along through the heat I could not but recall the rather odd talk we had with Custer on the evening of the twenty second. When officer's call was sounded we assembled at his bivouac and squatted in groups about his cot. He told us that he expected to encounter at least a thousand Indians, and that all precautions for a long campaign must be taken. He said that until further orders no trumpet calls would be sounded except in an emergency. General Terry had offered him the additional force of the Second Cavalry which he had declined, confident that the Seventh could handle the matter alone. He also declined the offer of Gatling guns, because they might hamper our movements through such a rugged country. We were cautioned to husband our mules and ammunition and, finally, he asked all officers to make any suggestions to him at any time. This struck us all as the strangest part of the meeting, for you know how dominant and self reliant he always was, and we left him with a queer sort of depression. McIntosh, Wallace, Godfrey and I walked back to our tents together and finally Wallace said—"I believe General Custer is going to be killed."

"Why?" asked Godfrey. "Because I never heard

him talk in this way before—that is, asking the advice of any one."

This was going through my mind during the five miles of march and then we saw clouds of dust about ten miles ahead of us so the column again halted and batallions were formed of three companies each, commanded by Reno, Yates, Keogh. Benteen's battalion which was composed of H, D, and K companies, was sent to the left about five miles to see if the Indians were trying to escape up the valley of the Little Big Horn, after which we were to hurry and rejoin the command as quickly as possible. We never saw Custer after that. He went on with the balance of the command and, when he got in sight of the village, he ordered Reno, with companies A, G, and M to cross the Little Big Horn and open the fight, while he kept to the right with companies C, E, F, I, and L, and would attack the village in another place, and all this time Tom McDougall with B company was about three miles in our rear, bringing up the pack mules. When we got within two miles of the village Benteen got a note from Cooke, which ran thus—"Come on—big village—be quick—bring packs." We didn't wait for the packs as we felt pretty sure no Indians had passed our rear.

When we reached the battleground we found utter confusion. Reno had made a charge and had been repulsed, and driven back, his three troops came riding back to us in disorder, and he at the head, without hat. It was in that charge that McIntosh and Benny Hodgson fell. We then joined our three companies with Reno's, put ourselves in position on a hill, and waited for McDougall to come up with the packs, and just before he reached us the Indians commenced to swarm around us like devils, thousands of them, all with modern rifles, while we were using old carbines, so we were put immediately on the defensive. We heard Custer's command fighting about five miles off in our front, and we tried repeatedly, but in vain, to join him. It was impossible as we could neither abandon our wounded men, nor the packs of the whole command. Reno ordered Weir to take his company and try to make connection with Custer, but he returned saying he could find no sign of Custer's command and that there were enough Indians there to eat up his company a hundred times over. Then our whole eight companies A, B, C, D, G, K, H and M went up to the highest point we could find, and with field glasses tried to locate Custer, but could see absolutely nothing, and finally concluded that he had gone to the timbers about six miles off and fortified himself. We found our present position hard to defend so we moved back to where we made our first stand. The Indians fought us until late that night. Of course no one dared close an eye, and at three o'clock in the morning, June twenty-sixth they opened fire on us again, harder than ever and all day long. It was oppressively hot and we were cut off from water, so the suffering was intense, especially among the wounded and dying. On the second day (the twenty-sixth) H company had three men killed and twenty one wounded. We occupied the most exposed position and the Indians had a clear fire at us from four sides, and my only wonder is that every one of us wasn't killed. The bullets fell like a perfect shower of hail, and every instant I thought I certainly would be the next struck. They got to making bold charges on us, and it took hard fighting to keep them from riding over us, and getting our stock. Along in the afternoon our position became so desperate and our force depleted so rapidly by killed and wounded that it became absolutely necessary to do something if we hoped to live through the day, so we rallied our men and made three successful dismounted charges on them in all of which the Indians lost heavily, so they thought it wise to give us a little wider berth. The effect produced on the savages encouraged our men greatly, and they commenced to take heart again. The enemy continued to fight us until about six o'clock that evening, after which we would hear occasional shots, but pretty soon the firing ceased entirely, and about seven o'clock their village and all hands moved out hastily in a southerly direction, going away from us and we began to breathe freely again. In all this time we had heard nothing of Custer so we concluded he had gone with General Terry. About nine o'clock on the evening of the twenty-sixth we were surprised to see Girard, the interpreter walk into our midst. He is the man you remember we used to buy eggs from. He had become separated from Reno's command, and concealed himself in the bushes right in the midst of the Indians through it all, and about twelve o'clock that night in walked de Rudio. You can imagine our delight at the sight of him, for of course every one supposed him to be dead. It would take too much time and paper to give you a detailed account of his narrow escapes and experiences—he will tell you all about it when he sees you. Well, that night you may depend upon it we slept well. About eight o'clock on the morning of the twenty seventh we saw clouds of dust arising about five miles in our front. We watched it steadily with glasses and soon saw a column advancing. Then the question arose as to whether they were Indians or soldiers. Some thought one way and some the other, so Reno sent some scouts out to ascertain, and in about half an hour they returned and said it was Terry with Gibbon's command. That explained the cause of the Indian's sudden departure the night before.

Can you imagine what a relief it was, and how grateful we felt when we saw these troops coming to succor us, absolutely taking us right out of the jaws of death, and such a horrible death. Of course, we inquired immediately for Custer and his five companies, and to our utter surprise and uneasiness we found that they had neither seen nor heard anything of them. H company was sent out over Custer's battle ground for further information and it was not until then that we had any positive knowledge of what had happened to them. There we found them all, over two hundred and fifty souls, every last man of them killed. We recognized all of the officers but Porter, Harrington, Jack Sturgis and Dr Lord. There is no hope of their having escaped for Porter's coat with his name in it was found with a bullet through the back, and we found Jack's pants, shirt and underwear with his name on them, but we could find no trace whatever of Harrington, or Dr Lord. It was the most horrible sight my eyes ever rested on. A Crow Indian who was with Custer, got a Sioux blanket and made his escape. He is the only living man we know who saw Custer fight. He says the troops fought desperately and killed more Indians than there were soldiers.

The Indians left their village to fight Custer and fought dismounted. The officers of Gibbon's command know this Crow Indian and say he is a truthful man. In our seven companies they killed and wounded about one hundred and twelve men and two officers.

On the twenty-seventh I buried McIntosh, and his grave is nicely marked. Benny Hodgson was also buried that day. Varnum cried over Benny's death like a baby—you know how much they thought of one another. Benteen also took Yates death very hard. On the twenty eight the command moved to Custer's battleground, and buried all the dead. I have been placed in command of C troop and my men buried Custer and Tom and their young schoolboy brother. I had them placed beside each other, and the graves marked.

Had Gibbon's command not come the Indians would not have left us, and it would only have been a question of time for them to get us all, for our ammunition would have given out, likewise our provisions, and we would have shared the same fate of the others. On the twenty-ninth everything the Indians had left in the village was destroyed by General Terry's orders. We made litters for the wounded and carried them many miles to the Far West, which was on the Big Horn, just at the mouth of the Little Big Horn. We then marched to the river and were put on this side of the Far West. Yesterday she went to Bismarck to get in telegraphic communication with General Sheridan, and we believe we are to remain in camp until her return, which will be in about two weeks. Smith of Terry's command went to Bismarck to attend to the business. General Terry with the balance of his staff are here. There never was such a Indian fight in this country before, and probably never will be again. Say nothing about what I am about to tell you, but if it hadn't been for Benteen every one of us would have been massacred. Reno did not know which end he was standing on, and Benteen just took the management of affairs in his own hands, and it was very fortunate for us that he did. I think he is one of the coolest and bravest men I have ever known.

Poor Mollie—her heart will be completely broken. . . .

The rest of the letter was purely personal. It slipped from my hands, and a torrent of tears en-

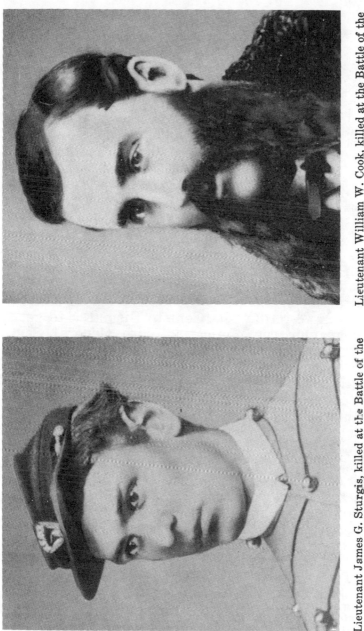

Lieutenant James G. Sturgis, killed at the Battle of the Little Bighorn.

Lieutenant William W. Cook, killed at the Battle of the Little Bighorn.

Lieutenant Henry M. Harrington, killed at the Battle of the Little Bighorn.

Lieutenant William Van W. Riley, killed at the Battle of the Little Bighorn.

Captain George W. Yates, killed at the Battle of the Little Bighorn.

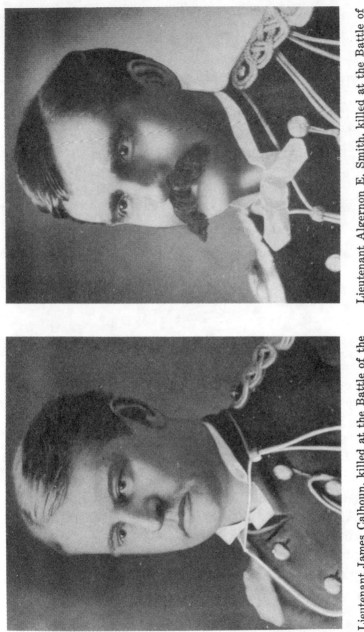

Lieutenant James Calhoun, killed at the Battle of the Little Bighorn.

Lieutenant Algernon E. Smith, killed at the Battle of the Little Bighorn.

gulfed me—tears mingled with grief and thankfulness—thankfulness for that unknown power
which, using me as its instrument, saved my husband's life, for what reason I knew not, neither
did I speculate upon why it did not send forth its
strange warning to Mollie and the others. But
perhaps that stage had already been set. Besides,
these mysteries are locked within the bosom of
some Divine Wisdom. Grief I had for my sister;
for Maggie Calhoun, so cruelly robbed of not only
husband, but her three brothers, and little Benny,
just a schoolboy who was spending his vacation
with them, and had begged so hard to be taken on
the expedition; for Mrs. Custer; for Annie Yates
with her three small children; and all the others.

My mind flashed back to that moonlight *fête
champêtre* not so many months ago, when all
seemed so happy and serene. I saw General Custer
stretched on the grass at the feet of his wife. I
saw boyish, freckle-faced Tom Custer, always
prowling, never still, and Lieutenant Calhoun, so
quiet and dignified, yet so full of real life and fun.
I saw handsome blond Captain Yates dancing with
his fairy-footed Annie. I saw Lieutenant Cook,
the Algernon Smiths, and that good-looking rogue,
Lieutenant Van W. Riley, only recently joined, and
Captain Keogh, and dark, romantic Lieutenant
Harrington, swallowing gallons of lemonade. I
thought of gay Benny Hodgson, playing mumblety-
peg in the moonlight. I thought of the charming
outsider, Lieutenant John Crittenden, of the Twentieth Infantry, who had been so eager to join the

expedition, and, of course, my mind dwelt long and lovingly upon my brother-in-law Donald, and all the rest of them, now lying in shallow graves on the plains.

I finally dried my eyes, picked up my letters, and went over to see Mrs. Benteen, where I found Mrs. de Rudio and the others, and here I spent the day.

Of course, after the massacre there followed a long chase to capture the Indians, and the warrior chiefs who led them in battle—chiefs Gall, Crow King, Black Moon, of the Uncpapa Sioux; Low Dog, Crazy Horse, Big Road, of the Ogallala Sioux; Spotted Eagle of the Sans-Arc Sioux; Tump of the Minneconjoux; and White Bull and Little Horse of the Cheyennes. To these belong the chief honors of conducting the fight, of whom, however, Gall, Crow King, and Crazy Horse were the ruling spirits.

List of Officers killed in the Battle of the Little Bighorn

Lieutenant Colonel George Armstrong Custer, Seventh U. S. Cavalry (addressed by his Civil War rank of General)

CAPTAINS
Thomas W. Custer
George W. Yates
Myles W. Keogh

LIEUTENANTS
Donald McIntosh
Algernon E. Smith

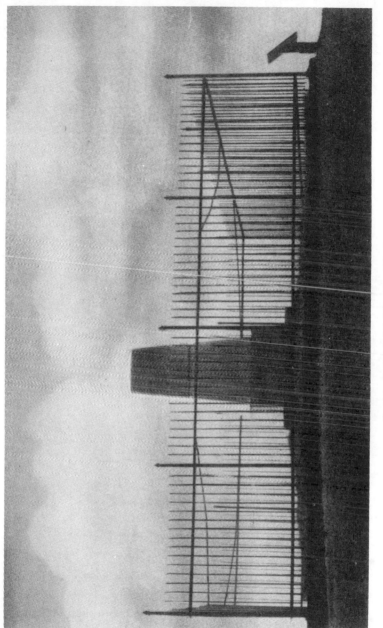

Custer Battlefield, Hardin, Montana.

Picture of the gold watch fob taken from Lieutenant Algernon Smith's body.

William W. Cook
James E. Porter
James Calhoun
Henry M. Harrington
James G. Sturgis
Benjamin H. Hodgson
William Van W. Riley
John J. Crittenden, Twentieth Infantry (attached
to L Troop, Seventh Cavalry)
Dr. George E. Lord (assistant surgeon, attached
to Custer's squadron)

All hopes of the immediate return of the troops
having vanished, the women of the regiment had
to swallow their disappointment, along with the
alkali dust and strained, cloudy water scooped up
from the Missouri mud flats, and, with Penelope
patience, sew and wait.

And how this little band clung together! Some
of us could have returned for a few months to
our family homes, but we chose to remain and
share everything, good or bad, that came to one
or all of us.

Bit by bit, gleaned from the infrequent letters
of our men, some pathetic instances of the disaster's aftermath seeped through to us. For exam-
ple, Captain Moylan retrieved from a back pocket
of Lieutenant Algernon Smith's trousers a gold
horse watch fob, overlooked in the Indians' hasty
pilfering of the bodies. This trinket, of small in-
trinsic value, had served as a sort of regimental
joke, which revolved around Lieutenants Smith

and Gibson. Frank had always admired the bauble, and about the mess table or campfire nights, Algy used to say, "Gib, if I'm killed first, I will the fob to you, and if you go first I get your bloodstone ring." Whereupon someone would shout, "And if you're both killed together, then who gets the loot?" and this would evoke loud claims and counterclaims, midst hearty laughter. However, when the jest became a grim reality, Mrs. Smith insisted upon presenting the fob to my husband, which he wore to the day of his death, and often as his hand strayed toward it, a detached, faraway look would creep into his eyes, followed by a sort of brooding silence as the past unfurled.

In the roundup of some of the Indians and squaws, Lieutenant Varnum picked up Jimmy Porter's knife from a young buck, and my husband caught sight of something glittering on the breast of a squaw. It was Benny Hodgson's gold watch case, from which the works had been removed, and which she was wearing as a locket.

Frank took it from her and, opening it, read with tears in his eyes the affectionate inscription accompanying this gift to Benny from his father upon the former's graduation from the Point. Later my husband returned it to the brokenhearted father.

Lieutenant Cook was one of the bravest men in the regiment, a crack shot, and had seen much service. The night before the massacre Frank was surprised to have him come into his tent and say,

Memorandum book taken from the body of Lieutenant McIntosh,
showing bullet hole.

"Gibby, this is my will, and I want you to witness it."

My husband laughed and retorted, "What, getting cold feet, Cookie, after all these years with the savages?"

"No," he answered, "but I have a feeling tha t the next fight will be my last."

"Oh, listen to the old woman," chaffed Jack Sturgis, flinging himself back on Frank's cot. "Bet he's been to see a fortune teller," and he chortled with amusement. How little they foresaw the tragic rendezvous that awaited them.

Lieutenant Hare took a notebook of Donald's from another squaw. He used to carry it inside his flannel shirt. It had a bullet hole right over his heart, showing that he had been killed instantly, thank God. The Indians were so near at the time that he was dragged right off his horse.

Comanche, pampered by every man, woman, and child of the regiment, survived the disaster many years. Free as air he roamed the hills and valleys, for no saddle girth nor bit ever cinched his flanks nor sawed his mouth again. He waxed fat and lazy upon sugar and tidbits, as well as the abundant grazing lands of the Black Hills and, later, those of Kansas, where he died.

There were many deeds of unrecorded valor performed during those tragic days. My husband was commanded to hold a very exposed position near a creek, the only source of water for miles around, and the wounded and dying were suffering from thirst. An Irish soldier asked permission to go into the ravine to fill the canteens. It seemed like running into the face of death, and Lieutenant Gibson, torn by the pitiful cries of the sufferers, simply said, "I could not order you to take such a risk."

"But I will take it, sir," replied the man, and, throwing himself on his stomach, he crawled through the tall grasses, replenished the canteens, and returned safely. This he did three times. His name was McDermott.

My first letter from Mrs. Custer in response to mine was pathetic and brief. It began:

My dearest Katie—.

Thank you for your loving sympathy which will help me in the dark days that are to follow. Later I hope to carry out Autie's wish and lay him to rest in the cemetery at West Point. Thank God your Frank was spared. Give him my love and tell him I will never forget him. I shall return to Monroe for a little while, and perhaps you will write some times to your devoted but desolate—

Elizabeth B Custer.

She clung to those who were left of the old Seventh to the end of her days, sistering the young widows and mothering the orphans of those gallant men who fell with Custer.

Well, we didn't see the troops for nine dreary months, and, of course, there was much rejoicing when they finally returned, tempered, too, with sadness over the tragedy and sympathy for those families who mourned.

However, as the ranks were refilled with

Captain Francis M. Gibson and his two Lieutenants, William Nicholson and George Cameron (both of whom became Generals). General Cameron is still living.

Mrs. Francis M. Gibson and Baby Kate.

straight-backed youngsters from the Point, and fresh enlisted men, and the regiment was transferred to its new headquarters at Fort Meade, Dakota, the sedative of time began to dim our somber memories. Yet certain wraiths of the past refused to be laid away, and they filtered through to our private lives bringing back visions of bygone days through strange channels.

Mollie had been so prostrated with grief that she recoiled from any further contact with the army until some years later when she suddenly changed her mind. The reason for it was the anticipated advent into this vale of tears of our first and, as fate decreed it, only child. When I received her wire announcing that she was already en route to join me, I mentally quailed, recalling her quaint antipathy to *boy* babies. "Champion bawlers and devilish brats," she dubbed them with a sniff. Suppose I had one! I pictured her figuratively slapping the unfortunate infant in the face with her sunbonnet, like Betsy Trotwood, and quitting us in high dudgeon. Anyway, she left the train at Fort Pierre and, in December 30 degrees below zero weather, battled by way of stagecoach through ice and snow to Fort Meade, arriving in time for the great event. However, when she gathered my two-and-a-half-pound baby girl in her capable arms, rolled her in an army blanket, and began issuing spritely orders to everyone, Frank included, I knew that all was well.

But to revert to the miracle of returning ghosts. Our wee one was barely two weeks old, and my husband, then a captain, was sitting in his barracks, when there came a knock on the door.

"Come in," he called, and a soldier entered.

"Beg pardon, sir," explained the man, saluting, "but there's an Indian outside from the Belle Fourche who insists upon seeing you."

The captain was surprised. "Is he armed?" he asked warily.

"No, sir."

"Then send him in and remain outside the door."

When the red man appeared, swathed from head to foot in buffalo skins, he was carrying a package under his arm.

The captain looked searchingly into his pockmarked face and queried, a bit suspiciously, "Who are you, and what do you want?"

The Indian placed his package on the end of the desk and replied slowly, "The captain not know Indian, but Indian know captain from back many moons."

The officer became curious. "When and where did you know me?"

"From time captain put Indian's squaw and papoose in wagon and gave them drink."

Then my husband's mind probed back to that steaming day when he brought some hostile prisoners back to Randall, and the young squaw had given birth to an infant on the prairie. Then this Indian had appeared utterly indifferent regarding the comfort of his family.

"Now I do remember," the captain admitted, "and I trust you are not stealing any more cattle."

This stalwart apparition of bygone days smiled slightly.

"No, no more steal. Indian is trapper now on Belle Fourche, and because captain help Indian's squaw and papoose, Indian bring present for captain's so small papoosie." Picking up the package from the desk, he unrolled from a torn piece of paper two beautiful little beaver skins. "These keep papoosie warm," he grunted. How this savage ever learned of our baby's arrival was a mystery. Frank was both touched and confused, and impulsively his hand went to his pocket and drew out a handful of silver.

"Why—why, thank you," he stammered, "and take this for your trouble."

But waving the money aside, the Indian drew himself up with quaint dignity.

"No, no sell skins. Indian *give* skins."

The captain reddened, then said quickly, "Well, thank you very much. But take off your coat and sit by the fire. You must be cold after such a trip."

The man nodded, slipped off his furs and, huddling close to the stove, rubbed his horny, chapped hands. Frank went to the door, opened it, and gave an order to the waiting soldier. Then he returned and, taking out his tobacco pouch, offered some of its contents to his visitor along with a pipe. This he accepted with alacrity and, filling the bowl, grunted and slunk back in his chair, smoking in complete contentment. There came another knock at the door, and this time the enlisted man entered with a tray of hot food from the soldiers' mess, consisting of plenty of buffalo meat, potatoes, a pint of coffee, and a whole pie made of dried apples. A smile of childish surprise wreathed the face of the red man, and, ignoring such culinary tools as knife and fork, he grabbed the meat in his fingers and sank his strong teeth into it, tearing the flesh from the bone. Everything else disappeared with celerity until nothing but crumbs remained.

When he had finished he pounded his protruding stomach, grunted, "Good," and accepted more tobacco. Fortunately a government wagon happened to be going towards the Belle Fourche that afternoon, so the Indian's pony, also well fed, was tied to the back of it, while its master rode inside until the roads forked.

In parting the captain said, gripping the rough hand in a warm clasp, "Again let me thank you for your gift. Also my squaw thanks you, and may the Great Spirit prosper you and bring you good hunting."

Thus the bread that my husband cast upon the waters years before was returned to him. Good use we made of the furs, for we stowed our mite of humanity between them. When she outgrew them we made them into rugs.

Of course my family was clamoring for a picture of the baby, but I hesitated to send one for two reasons: first, because she was such a scrap, and, secondly, because her hair simply wouldn't grow. It was so long in coming in that I feared she was going to be bald, then I discovered that it had sprouted, so to speak, but was so fine that

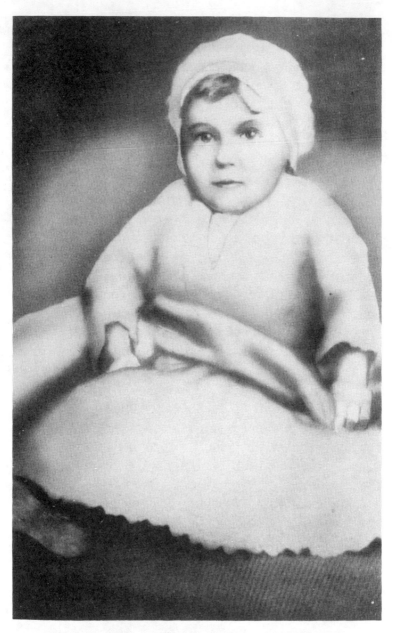

Baby Kate Gibson, wearing a curl of General Custer's.

you could scarcely see it, since it was almost white.

Meantime, as the months rolled by, my lady-mother's letters not only grew more insistent regarding a photograph, but she was becoming vaguely alarmed. What was the matter with the child? Was she cross-eyed, crippled, queer? I was in a quandary what to do, and then one day the problem solved itself.

I happened to be rummaging through an old trunk that hadn't been used for ages, and, quite by chance, my hand fell upon a small box. Wonderingly, I opened it, and as I did so I caught my breath, for another shade of the long ago was released to haunt me—a beneficent shade—a shade that revived a merry jest, made one day at Fort Lincoln.

Yes, looking up at me almost challengingly, as though daring me to blot out the past, lay the forgotten golden curl of General Custer. At first sight of it, bringing its poignant memories, I was threatened with an attack of hysterics, but I fought to control myself—I had to for Mollie's sake. Then, after a while, as I calmed down an idea came to me, and, taking one of the lace caps my husband's mother had sent the baby, I basted that curl in the front of it, and thus my wee one's first picture was taken. Mollie's reaction to the incident was less violent than I had expected, for she had settled back into the old life again—a willing prisoner, held by tiny hands and the voice of Baby Kate lisping, "My Auntie Tosh." In fact, she might have clung to her Western moorings indefinitely, if an urgent telegram announcing the critical illness of our lady-mother had not sent us both hurrying back to Washington.

The most tangible and perpetual ghost of those stirring days abides in Kansas, where the regiment was anchored for many years. Here the mounted carcass of Comanche, reverently presented by the soldiers to the state, holds and focuses the awed interest of adventurous youth and students of history alike upon the never-to-be-forgotten Battle of the Little Bighorn.

So time passes. Donald and Mollie lie side by side near my husband in the National Cemetery at Arlington, just at the entrance of Fort Myer. The latter, retired for physical disability incurred during his years of hard service, explained the selection of this particular location thus, "Because Donald and I will always be within sound of the trumpet calls we loved." And here, someday, in this beautiful, peaceful spot, I, too, will rest, happy in the knowledge that all around me and mine are sleeping many dear old friends.

Today, in jaunty modern uniforms, the Seventh Cavalry is garrisoned in the great Southwest, at Fort Bliss, Texas. Here, realizing that eventually every branch of the service will be swept into the maw of complete motorization, the regiment clings a little longer to its best friend—the passing horse. Here, also, the organization cherishes its records of the past and still holds high the torch of patriotism and military efficiency lighted for it by Custer and his soldiers of yesteryear.

Sometimes as I sit by the window watching the glowing sunset, I seem to feel the hand of my sister slip into mine on one side of me, and that of Elizabeth Custer in the other. Together we vision again, vanishing over the horizon into the gathering twilight, dust-covered, obsolete uniforms and cavalry caps, above purposeful phantom faces, and swaying bodies astride spectral, big-boned horses, trumpet-call conscious. We glory in the honor of having shared in the lives of such. No paeans of praise are sung over their forgotten graves—many unmarked. None are needed. No tempestuous huzzas ring out from hysterical crowds, no wreaths are hurled beneath their shadowy feet, yet we who lived with and among these dauntless souls, lift our hearts in silent pride and gratitude:

To the soldiers in blue and black campaign hats,
To the trumpet and carbine and obsolete gat,
To those fighting men cast in Uncle Sam's mold,
Who safeguarded the railroads and settlers of old.